'A Fair and High Locality'

The Chronicle of
Coombe Ridge House
and
'The Manor of Coombe'

Childhood Home of John Galsworthy Set in the Historic Surrey Estate

By Sue Lown and Patricia Panizzo

Illustrated by Ian Dunn

Limited Edition. Copy Number: 468

First published 1996 by
PWP Press,
172 Coombe Lane West,
Kingston, Surrey. KT2 7DE

ISBN 0 9528594 0 8

Printed and bound for PWP Press by Roseheath Printing & Co., Vitalia House, Wood Lane, Hemel Hempstead, Hertfordshire. HP2 4TF Tel: 01442 216941

There are many people that we need to thank for their help, time, support and encouragement. Firstly, Ian Dunn, for his truly delightful illustrations and Les Kirkin for his help with original and reproduction photography.

We would also like to express our gratitude to Sister Sheila Brennan, Sister Provincial and the Sisters of the Holy Cross, as well as Mrs M K Hayes, Head Teacher of Holy Cross Preparatory School. We also must thank the past and present Sister Provincials of the Congregation of the Holy Family of Villefranche de Rouergue for their assistance and the loan of their beautiful collection of photographs.

We are also grateful to Tim Everson, Local History Officer for his assistance and advice, as well as Jill Lamb, Assistant Archivist and Paul Hill, Curator at Kingston Museum for their patience. Our thanks also go to Martin Higgins, Senior Planning Assistant for the Royal Borough of Kingston Upon Thames for his detailed knowledge and advice. The National Monuments Record Office in Swindon and The Royal Commission on Historical Monuments of England in London have been a great help and the Reprographics Department at the Public Records Office at Kew deserve a special mention for their assistance.

Naturally, we could not have even started our publication without consulting the excellent books and articles that have already been written. Therefore we would also like to particularly thank June Sampson, Shaan Butters, Anne McCormack, the late Joan Wakeford, L E Gent, and J W Lindus Forge. Last but not least, John Galsworthy himself!

We have also used numerous other sources, too many to mention here; these have been credited at the back of the book.

Dedication:

For Paolo, Virginia, Dominic, Becky, Valentina and Grace: our children.

Woman and child along Coombe Lane West in the early 1900's near to Coombe Farm.

Coombe Ridge House was built on land which was once rough pastureland belonging to this farm.

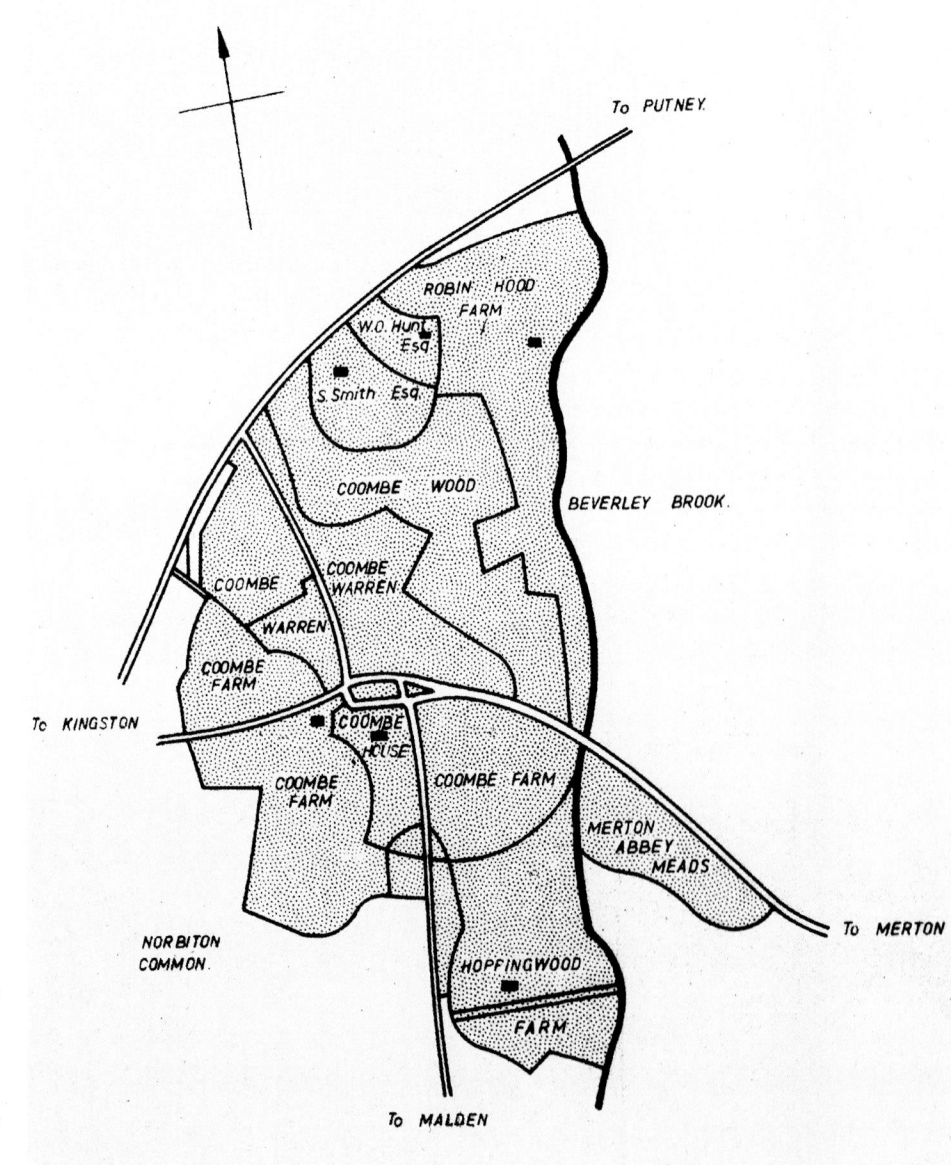

This map shows the extent of the ancient Coombe Manor Estate when it was sold by Earl Spencer to the first Duke of Cambridge.

At the time the holding consisted of some c1300 acres, with three farms and only three houses.

The Duke and later his son the second Duke were to considerably increase the size of the estate.

Contents

An illustration showing the dilapidated Ivy Conduit House as it appears today, in the grounds of Coombe Ridge House. Built in c1515 by Cardinal Wolsey as part of an ingenious fresh water supply to Hampton Court Palace, this ancient Grade II scheduled monument was badly damaged by a V1 bomb which fell nearby during the Second World War.

We started to write this book in the Summer of 1994, after we had helped the Year 6 girls of Holy Cross Preparatory School to research and then paint a large Mural which depicts the history of Kingston, Coombe and Coombe Ridge House. It now adorns the School's Dining Room wall and was awarded Joint First Prize in the Kingston Schools Environmental Award Scheme for 1995.

Whilst researching the history of Coombe Ridge House and the Coombe area we became intrigued with the story of the Ivy (or Bush) Conduit, the little well-house in the grounds of the school. Despite being an English Heritage Grade II Scheduled Monument there appear to be no pre-war plans or photographs which depict what this building originally looked like, before it was damaged by a bomb in 1944. It fell into further disrepair in the 1950's, when the Tudor lead sinks were stolen and since then it has been left, as its name implies, to become overgrown with the ivy bushes that surround it.

As we had already trawled all the libraries and archives that might possibly have had pictures - to no avail - we decided to contact as many of the living descendants of past owners of Coombe Ridge House as we could, in the hope that they might have a photograph showing the little well house. Every family we did contact has been enormously helpful and offered every support, but sadly to date a picture has not materialised.

During the course of our research however, we came across some old maps of the Hampton Court Water supply, which as far as we know have never been published.

These maps give us a little more information on the course of the system and how the water may have been collected, but regrettably, they only show the floorplans of the conduit houses and not the elevations of the buildings.

We will be continuing our investigations, as we live in hope that someone, somewhere may have further evidence which will finally enable the Ivy Conduit House to be restored to its former glory.

It is our intention to use some of the proceeds from this publication as a foundation for a Preservation Fund, which will at least enable a full archaeological survey and maintenance work to proceed on what is one of the oldest buildings in the Coombe area.

We hope that this book will be of interest to anyone who has associations with Holy Cross School, the families who lived in the house, or anyone who knows, loves or lives in the Coombe area itself.

**Sue Lown
and
Patricia Panizzo
June 1996**

"*Selecting a fair and high locality, not too far away from London, he set himself at once to make a country place, where the little things should have fresh air, new milk and all the fruit of the earth home-grown around them. Quite wonderful was the forethought he lavished on that house and little estate stretching down the hill*".

John Galsworthy (1867-1933), who was awarded the Nobel Prize for literature in 1932.

The author was born on nearby Kingston Hill, and spent his childhood in Coombe.

This evocative description of a wealthy Victorian father choosing a site for a country house was written in 1910 by John Galsworthy in 'A Portrait'. In this work the author drew directly upon the recollections of his own father, who in the 1860's came in search of land upon which to build a home. The family were to live here for the next 18 years in three adjoining properties along George Road.

Coombe Ridge House (which they called 'Coombe Leigh') was to be their favourite house and the place where the Galsworthy children spent much of their happy childhood.

Since the Galsworthy's left Coombe Ridge House in 1886 it has been home to several other eminent people and their families. The grounds too have been witness to many events, from lively garden parties to tranquil convent life and from the noise and destruction of wartime bombing to the happy sounds of today, as the children of Holy Cross Preparatory School play in the tree-filled garden.

Yet the story of Coombe Ridge House does not begin with the building of the 'little estate', as the Coombe area in which the house stands also has a unique and fascinating history. In the dawn of civilisation ancient man visited and later built a settlement on the hill. The Domesday Book recorded a small holding here known as 'Comb' and by Mediaeval times the lands were part of a Manorial Estate, which was to change hands several times over the following centuries.

Many noteworthy events took place locally including gruesome executions, bustling fairs and a notorious 'Battle' in which no blood was shed! Several renowned Coombe landowners, residents and visitors have not only influenced the history of the area, but have also had a wider part to play in national and international affairs.

Therefore, to set the house in its geographical and historical context, we will be looking closely at Coombe's recorded past, as well as outlining in detail the story of Coombe Ridge House - John Galsworthy's 'country place' in 'A Fair and High Locality'.

"In those days, Coombe was very different - much as I described it in the opening of the 'Man of Property".

(Letter from John Galsworthy to the 'Surrey Comet' in 1929).

The most famous work by John Galsworthy, 'The Forsyte Saga', is a collection of books, commencing with 'The Man of Property' which tells the story of several generations of a wealthy middle-class family.

It was based in part on some of the characters, events and places in the author's own life, including his childhood home of Coombe; the inspiration for the setting of the fictitious 'Robin Hill'.

The 'Saga' was televised four times by the BBC and in 1969, when it was first shown on BBC1, it was estimated that nearly 16 million people watched the 26-episode series. It has also been viewed by countless audiences world-wide and is still considered by some to be one of the finest TV adaptations of a literary work.

This picture is taken from the 1960's BBC Production.

Here John Bennett, who played the architect Phillip Bosinney, is showing Nyree Dawn Porter, who starred as Irene Forsyte, the house he was building for her husband Soames, at 'Robin Hill'.

The hill on which Coombe Ridge House stands today was formed gradually over hundreds of thousands of years. As the River Thames was pushed southwards during successive Ice Ages, it left in its wake fertile flood plains, surrounded by high land. Thus Coombe/Kingston Hill came into creation.

There is evidence to indicate some form of primitive human life here from as long as 300,000 years ago, as a hand axe, possibly dating from the Lower Palaeolithic era, has been found on the slopes of the hill. Much later, during the New Stone Age which was around 5,500 years ago, a group or tribe of nomadic hunters possibly passed through, leaving behind polished axes, arrowheads and pottery, all of which have been found nearby.

The first evidence we have of people actually living on the hill dates from the Bronze Age, around 3,000 years ago and it is believed that there was once a large village situated on what is now Coombe Wood Golf Course, opposite Coombe Ridge House. (These settlements were often sited on well-drained south-facing slopes, near to a fresh water supply).

The ancient Coombe settlers grew crops and kept cattle and sheep for meat. Presumably they also used the wool for weaving, as a large loom weight was found in the vicinity (this is today displayed in the British Museum). They were also bronze metal workers and from the many items which have been discovered we can assume that the village was a thriving community.

Furthermore it has been surmised that at a later date there was once a Roman villa or settlement somewhere on the hill. Some limited evidence has been found to support this theory, including coins, urns, pottery and other artefacts. An account by the Tudor topographer Leland mentioned that walls and foundations were discovered near to a gravel pit and the gallows (at one time possibly sited near to Coombe Ridge House). However this location has never been accurately identified.

Documentation dating from Mediaeval times also referred to a Romano-British settlement called 'Waleport', which was thought to have existed somewhere around Galsworthy Road, but more recent excavations around the area have not substantiated these claims. It could be that some of the alleged 'finds' may have been wrongly attributed to the Roman period by earlier historians and were actually Bronze Age in origin.

Whatever their origin, many of the artefacts that were reportedly found here have unfortunately 'disappeared' - such as the hoard of coins dating from the 3rd/4th century which were reputedly found near Golf Club Drive in the late 1700's and a bronze Roman statue also said to have been found in the vicinity in Victorian times.

Later farming and building developments have possibly destroyed any firm evidence which could tell us why the Romans were in Coombe. One possible theory for the items that have been allegedly discovered is that they were unrecovered buried treasure. Another delightful idea is that the coins and other valuables were left as 'offerings' to some ancient spring-water gods, but it is possible that we may never know.

However there are on-going archaeological investigations being carried out all the time and in 1986 Coombe was designated an 'Area of Archaeological Interest'.

The scene on Coombe Hill some 3,000 years ago. In the distance is the River Thames, which was a major trading route for the metals and other goods produced by the settlement. The ancient Coombe dwellers would have hunted for game and collected firewood from the dense woodlands as well as using the waters from the abundant springs nearby.

11

The first 'recorded' mention of the area known today as Coombe was in the Domesday Book written in 1086, when 'Comb' consisted of a few small tenanted farms. In 1215 King John granted the lands of Coombe to Hugh de Nevil and from this time the area was referred to as the Manor of Coombe Nevill. By the 1360's it is believed that there was a moated manor house somewhere in Coombe, but its exact location has never been identified.

Over the next few centuries, depending on the whims and fortunes of successive owners, Coombe Manor was to change hands several times and in the early 1500's it was owned by Merton Priory. At that time the head of the Catholic Church in England was Cardinal Wolsey, a man of great influence and wealth.

In 1514 he commissioned the building of a magnificent new palace at Hampton Court on the River Thames. The palace needed to have a good fresh-water supply and on Coombe Hill, some 5 kilometres away, his engineers found an ideal source. (The spring waters of Coombe were supposed to have restorative properties, which must have been a great attraction to the Cardinal as it was said that he suffered from 'stones').

He instigated a huge and costly engineering project to pipe the water to his palace using a gravity-feed system of underground lead pipes. The water was channelled down Coombe Hill, through Kingston near to the Fairfield, underneath both the Hogsmill and Thames Rivers. From there the pipes ran across the parkland and finally into the Palace kitchens.

On Coombe Hill, three Conduit (or well) Houses were built to control the supply of the water, as well as several 'tamkins' (access and maintenance points) along the way. (Maps dating from the mid-1700's also show that the Conduit Houses had large brick-built 'feeder' channels leading into them, which presumably collected supplementary surface rain water, but we do not know whether these 'feeders' are original or a later addition).

The well-houses are now the oldest buildings in the area, protected by Grade II scheduling. Coombe Conduit on Coombe Lane West and Gallows Conduit, in the grounds of a house in George Road, have been partially restored in recent years. Ivy (Bush) Conduit, which is in the grounds of Coombe Ridge House, was badly damaged by a V1 bomb in 1944. Further destruction occurred in the 1950's when the Tudor lead sinks were stolen.

Coombe springs were not the only water supply to the Palace, as by the 1630's the Longford River had been diverted to supplement the system. However Coombe water was still being piped there until the latter half of the last century and evidence suggests that all three Conduit Houses and the pipelines had been repaired regularly up until this time. The maintenance was costly and as the land under which the pipes ran was developed, the water became contaminated and access for repair difficult. The pipes which ran under the Thames were damaged by boats and by 1876 the Coombe supply was no longer used.

In 1895 the three Conduit Houses were sold to the Duke of Cambridge for £75.00 and the supply was officially terminated at the end of the last century, when many of the lead pipes were sold.

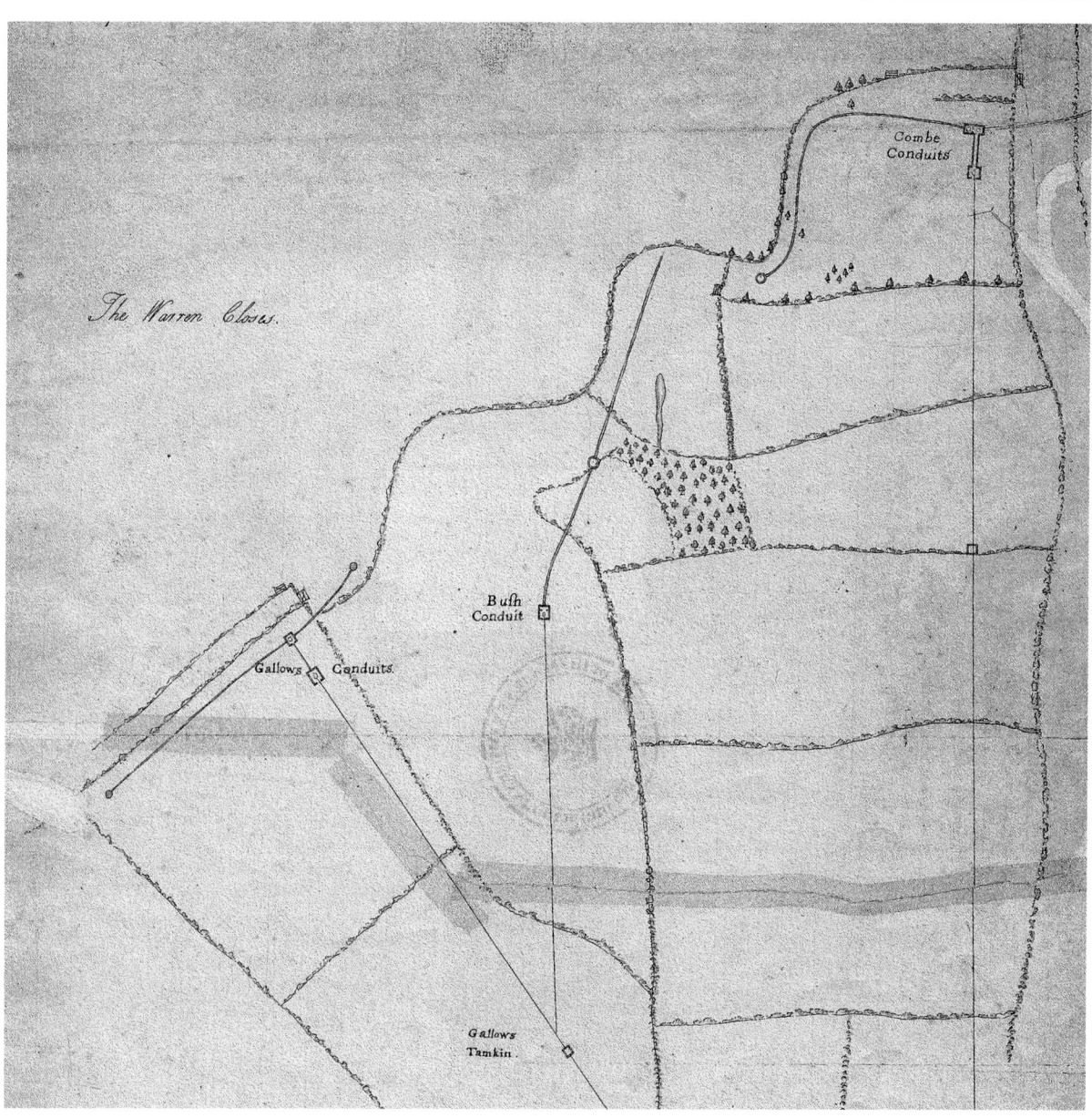

The Warren Closes.

Coombe
Conduits

Gallows Conduits.

Bush
Conduit

Gallows
Tamkin.

What is interesting about this map is that it clearly shows that the brick-built feeder pipes or gullies which ran into the three Conduit Houses were not connected to each other across the hilltop, as was shown on later mid 1800's maps. The pipes from the three Conduit Houses only came together at Norbiton, much further down the hill.

The little circles indicated on the feeder pipes are possibly small reservoirs and we know from later documentation that there was a deep culvert which ran underneath Coombe Lane, on the top right-hand side of the map. Digging work in the 1890's discovered that this culvert was 4'10" high by 2'6" wide, (147cms x 76 cms) presumably big enough for a man to walk through.

Much of the pipeline system ran under private land and some of the landowners were paid an annual rental of 'Two fat bucks and two does' - venison culled from the Royal parks.

All of these feeder pipes have now disappeared, presumably as a result of all the building and redevelopment of the George Road/Coombe Lane West areas.

Map dating from the mid - 1700's which shows the three Coombe Conduit Houses and Tamkin. Bush, or as it is here 'Bufh' Conduit is today in the grounds of Coombe Ridge House.

Coombe Conduit House originally consisted of two buildings joined by a tunnel, but the upper house was partially destroyed by a land mine during the Second World War and later further damaged by a falling tree.

In the 1930's, a lady called Mrs Hwfa Williams wanted to bottle and sell the water from Coombe Conduit, which was by then situated in the grounds of her house, Coombe Springs (now the site for Lord Chancellor Walk).

Unfortunately investigations at the time showed that the water was unfit for human consumption, possibly because of the high mineral content. (It was said that before the supply was discontinued, the water had not been used for many years at Hampton Court for cooking purposes, as it turned the vegetables black!)

In 1970 Coombe Conduit still issued spring water at the rate of 20 gallons per hour, but no further attempts have been made to utilise the once-coveted supply.

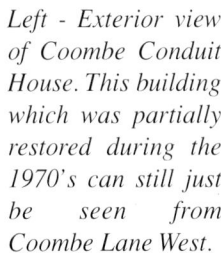

Left - Exterior view of Coombe Conduit House. This building which was partially restored during the 1970's can still just be seen from Coombe Lane West.

Right - Gallows Tamkin, now on Coombe Wood Golf Course. This was one of several access or maintenance points in the system.

Interior of Coombe Conduit showing the lead sink and entrance to the other chamber.

These photographs, taken in 1955, show the interior and exterior views of Ivy Conduit House. It is believed that a later tiled roof was added to the original vaulted roof in Victorian times, possibly to 'match' the main house. Today it is difficult to discern the roof as the whole area is covered with the ubiquitous ivy.

When preservation work starts one of the first jobs will be to carefully clear this ivy away in order that a proper site survey can be made. Much of the original Tudor brickwork was blown away when the V1 bomb fell nearby in 1944, although it is possible that some of the original fabric is buried in the nearby undergrowth.

It is possible to make out the remnants of the lead piping at the back of the building - where the water supply entered the Conduit House - although the two Tudor lead sinks were stolen shortly before these photos were taken.

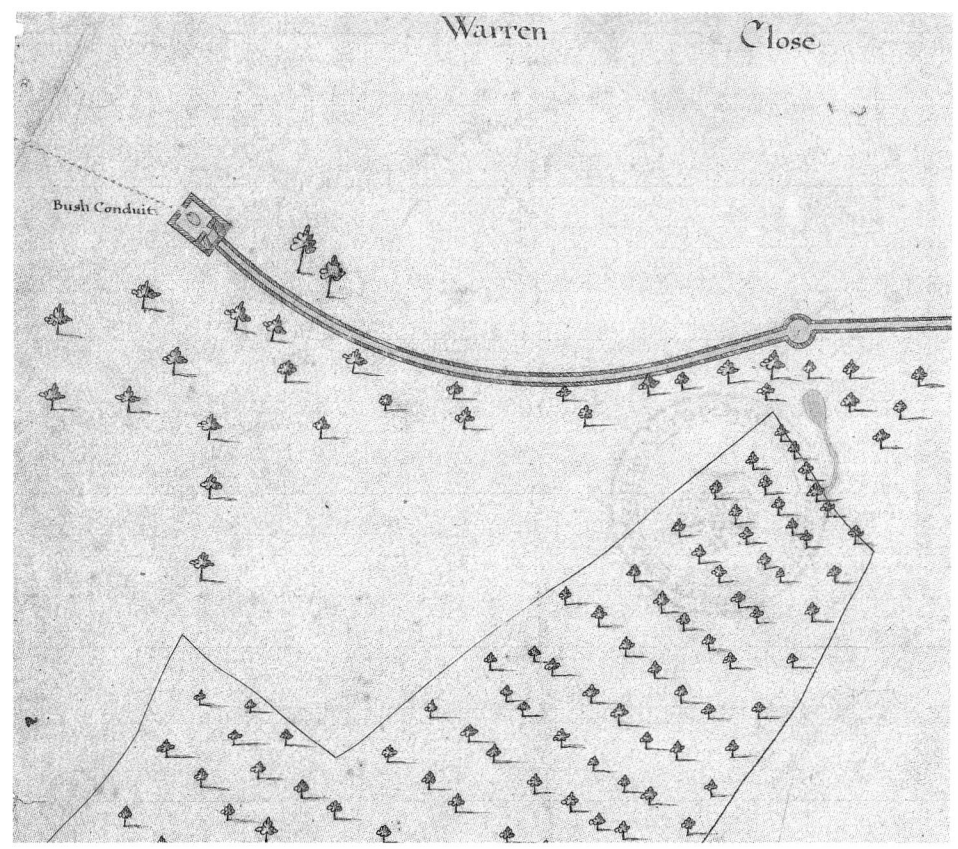

A map which probably dates from the mid 1700's which shows the floor plan and feeders for Bush (Ivy) Conduit House.

In 1537 King Henry VIII seized the assets of the Catholic Church in England during the dissolution of the monasteries and Coombe Manor and estate passed into the hands of the Crown. (Twelve years earlier the King had also taken possession of Wolsey's Hampton Court Palace. This also presumably included the services of the Conduit Houses).

In 1579, his daughter Elizabeth I granted Coombe to a favourite, Sir Thomas Vincent and he built a fine brick manor house at the top of what is now Traps Lane/Coombe Lane West. At the time this was one of the largest establishments in the Kingston district and Coombe was to be honoured by a visit from the great Queen herself in 1602.

Robert Banks Jenkinson (1770-1828) second Earl Liverpool.

The original Tudor house has long since gone but part of the wall which once surrounded the grounds can still be seen today along Traps Lane and Warren Rise.

The Manor was to change hands several times over the next two centuries. Subsequent owners included the Lord Mayor of London, Sir William Cockayne and John (later Earl) Spencer, an ancestor of Diana, Princess of Wales, who bought the estate in 1753.

The Tudor Manor House had to be rebuilt following a fire and the new Georgian mansion built on its site was leased by Earl Spencer to several prominent peers. (When road journeys were difficult, travellers could reach London via the River Thames from Kingston).

Possibly the most famous tenant of the house was Robert Banks Jenkinson, later Earl Liverpool, the long-serving British Prime Minister. He was premier from 1812 until 1827, and lived in the house - which he called Coombe Wood House - from 1802 until his death in 1828. He was married twice and, after her death, his first wife Louisa was commemorated in a statue which once adorned the entrance hall to Coombe Wood House. This statue is today in All Saints Church in Kingston.

Whilst he lived in Coombe many important and influential people visited him here, including Emperor Alexander of Russia, the King of Prussia and the Duke of Wellington on his way to the Battle of Waterloo. In 1805 there was great excitement when King George III came to dine, after reviewing his troops on Wimbledon Common. His entourage dined on venison on the beautiful lawns, whilst the King was lavishly entertained in Coombe (Wood) House.

One interesting fact from this time is that Sir John Soane, the world famous architect who designed the Bank of England, supervised many of the decorations and building works in Coombe (Wood) House. Although Soane was not the original architect on the house, he designed many of the internal and external features, including a new library and conservatory, as well as supervising several of the more mundane alterations. He worked here from 1785 until 1828, firstly for Wilbraham Tollemache (who later became Earl Dysart) and also for Lord Liverpool, with whom he became a personal friend.

In the 1770's Earl Spencer altered the road in front of Coombe House (Coombe Lane West) possibly because it ran too close to the new house. The diverted road curved around the grounds of the property, thus creating a larger garden at the front.

Today the small triangular piece of land at the top of Traps Lane denotes the lines of both the old and 'new' roads. (See also the Estate Map on page 4). The name Traps Lane itself probably dates from around this time, as the land next to and below the Manor House is shown on the old Spencer Estate Maps as having belonged to a 'Madam Trap'.

Left c1900 photo and below c1819 drawing by the architect Sir John Soane of the rear view of Coombe (Wood) House.

This beautiful Georgian house was built on the site of the old Tudor Manor in the 1750's.

17

In 1837, the third Earl Spencer sold the whole of the 1300-acre Coombe Estate to Prince Adolphus Frederick, son of George III, the first Duke of Cambridge. By then the Estate consisted of the tenanted Coombe House and grounds, three further tenanted farms and the ground leases on two other properties on Kingston Hill - Kenry House and Coombe Hurst.

From this time on the Estate ceased to be called the Manor of Coombe and in later years the Duke of Cambridge was to greatly enlarge the size of the Estate by buying adjacent land in Kingston and Norbiton. This practice continued when his son George, the second Duke, inherited Coombe in 1850. Like the Spencers, the Dukes of Cambridge did not live at Coombe House, although they took an active interest in local affairs.

After the death of Lord Liverpool, Coombe House was for a short time a boarding school with 27 pupils, run by the Reverend Biber. In 1847 it again became a private residence when John Sim (a landowner, JP and merchant) leased the house and 39 acres of land.

Once again Coombe welcomed a reigning monarch, as Queen Victoria was a regular visitor. It was said that she was very fond of Coombe House and part of the garden near the lake was afterwards always called 'Queen's Walk' in her honour. This lake can still be seen today near to Coombe House Chase.

By 1880 Coombe House had become a luxurious sanatorium providing water-based cures to wealthy socialites. Amongst the treatments offered by the proprietor, Doctor T E Foster MacGeogh, were Turkish and vapour baths, needle baths and other remedies. Perhaps like Cardinal Wolsey, the in-patients of Coombe House may have found the local waters efficacious!

In later years, several other families were to live there and in the early 1900's the grounds of the house were used as a venue for the Coombe and Malden Flower Shows and several fetes and fairs, which were always very well attended by the local population. By 1915, during the First World War, the owners were Doctor and Mrs Pearson. Sadly they were amongst the 1400 people killed when the Cunard Liner, the Lusitania, was torpedoed.

Coombe and Malden Flower Show in 1909.

Several well-attended fetes and flower shows were held in the spacious grounds of Coombe House in the early years of the twentieth century.

By the 1930's the once grand Coombe (Manor) House had become too costly to maintain. Many of the famous fixtures and fittings were sold at auction and the house was finally demolished in 1933.

There is little evidence today to denote the site of what was once an important Manor House save for a few of the outhouses and the two lodge-houses which have been converted into private homes.

All of the grounds have now been built over by the houses around Neville and Fitzgeorge Avenues.

These 1921 photographs show some interior views of Coombe House and are part of a collection of photographic plates taken by the father and son partnership of Bedford Lemere.

They show just some of the many sumptuous rooms. Above is a staircase and hallway, left a 'Boudoir' and below the Conservatory or 'Winter Garden'

The Warren: Gallows, Gatherings and Game

Above the Manor House, on the plateau of Coombe Hill were large tracts of dense woodland and open heathland known locally as 'The Warren'. John Galsworthy in "A Man of Property" later described it as being:

".. as lonely as a prairie, its silence only broken by the rustle of rabbits bolting to their holes, and the song of the larks."

Today a large part of this area is covered by Coombe Hill and Coombe Wood Golf Courses as well as some exclusive housing developments, yet for many centuries The Warren had been a wild and uninhabited place.

It was here that the owners of the Manor hunted the abundant game and their servants collected firewood. Local people often used the ancient tracks which led across the top of the hill as a shortcut and The Warren was also a place for public gatherings. For centuries it became the venue for both sombre and happy events.

On a site on the edge of the Warren near to Coombe Ridge House there were gallows, which for many years were used to publicly execute 'criminals'. The exact location of this hanging place is not known, and it is probable that it may have been sited at different places on the hill over the years. The map which dates from the mid-1700's on page 25 shows a gallows near to what is today Kingsnympton Estate however earlier Tudor reports indicate that they were possibly located on Coombe Wood Golf Course, opposite Coombe Ridge House.

There are several theories to support this idea. The Conduit House nearby has, as far as we know, always been called 'Gallows Conduit' and some old maps have traditionally referred to this area as 'Gallows Hill'. So although we cannot place the gallows exactly we do know that they were very nearby.

In 1588 a Catholic priest, William Way, was brought to Kingston to face his death, probably on either the gallows on Kingston Hill or The Warren. His 'crime' was that he had refused to deny his faith and accept Queen Elizabeth I as head of the Church in England. Father Way was captured and tried at Southwark in London, brought along the river by boat and then dragged (drawn) up Kingston Hill to be hung and quartered. He is revered today as 'Blessed William Way' by the Catholic Church; a title which is given to someone who has, in an outstanding way, lived or died for God.

In later years The Warren resounded with the noise of cheering and bloodthirsty crowds, when it was the venue for bull, cock and bare-fist fighting. Despite this not all the public events held here were so violent. Families also came to picnic and attend fairs and other festive gatherings. On Derby Day hundreds of excited racegoers swarmed across the heathland on their way to Epsom.

There has been a public house on the edge of the Coombe Estate on Kingston Hill for hundreds of years.

Originally called the Fox and Coney and later the George and Dragon, this coaching Inn was frequented by local people attending the fairs and executions on The Warren.

Today this building is part of the Kingston Lodge Hotel.

T he Warren has also played a small part in the history of Naval Communications when, in 1821, Earl Spencer sold a small piece of high land on the Warren for £100 to the Admiralty as a site for a Semaphore Station. This was part of an ingenious signalling system that was used for a number of years to enable the Admirals and Naval Commanders in Whitehall to send and receive messages from the Fleet in Portsmouth. The Semaphore Station has long since gone but a house later built opposite the site was called 'Telegraph Cottage' as a reminder.

This property was also to achieve renown as the war-time home to General Eisenhower. (See pages 49 and 51). It was demolished after a fire in 1987 and a new development, also called Telegraph Cottage, was built on the same site.

THE SEMAPHORE

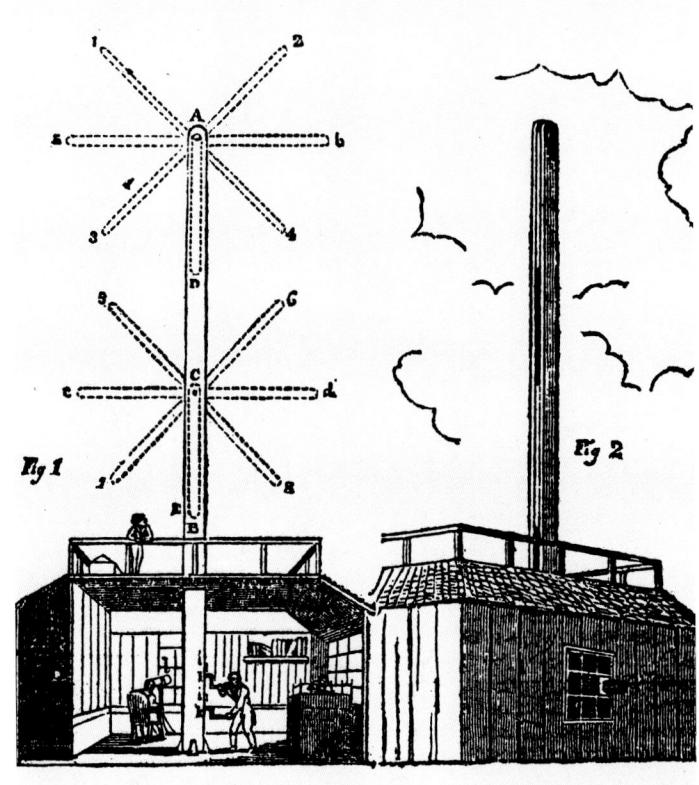

Above is an illustration of an old London to Portsmouth 'B' Type signalling station, similar to the Semaphore Station on Coombe Warren.

Admiralty to Portsmouth Semaphore Line 1822-1847

Each station was allocated to a Lieutenant on half-pay, to act as caretaker.

ADMIRALTY
London CHELSEA
PUTNEY HEATH
COOMBE WARREN
COOPERS HILL
CHATLEY HEATH
Guildford PEWLEY HILL
Godalming BANNICLE HILL
HASTE HILL
HOLDER HILL
Petersfield
THE BEACON
Southampton COMPTON DOWN
PORTSDOWN HILL
PORTSMOUTH Magazine LUMPS FORT
SPITHEAD
Portsmouth

N

NOT TO SCALE

Left is a map which shows the system of Semaphore Stations from the Admiralty-to-Portsmouth line, which was used for several years in the early 1800's. Coombe Station was the third along from Whitehall.

Illustration of the Scarce Dagger Moth, which was indigenous to Coombe Woods and became extinct in 1956.

In Victorian times these woods were visited by many keen lepidopterists looking for this and other rare specimens.

By the end of the 18th century Kingston was a major stopping place along several coaching routes, one of which was the old London to Portsmouth turnpike road.

As this road passed across the top of Coombe Hill the notorious, handsome young villain Jerry Abershaw, known as 'The Coombe Wood Highwayman', lay in wait for the unsuspecting travellers. Here he robbed them and then used the cover of the dense woods to escape.

Eventually, in 1795, Jerry was caught, tried and hung on Kennington Common and his body displayed on a gibbet at Kingston Vale. Thousands of people came to see the gruesome remains of the infamous and debonair brigand.

In 1850 The Warren was the subject of a notorious court case which was reported nationally in 'The Times' as 'The Battle of Coombe Warren'. At the time the affair caused a sensation as it challenged the right of a landowner - a Royal Prince no less - over the access rights on his own land.

His Royal Highness, the first Duke of Cambridge and owner of the Coombe Estate had decided to block off the public access across his land and thus stop the public from using the ancient and well-used Warren tracks as a shortcut. The Duke had guarded gates constructed at either end of what is today Warren Road, stating that although he was still willing to let 'respectable' people through 'all and sundry' would frighten the wildlife and spoil his shooting!

The local population were divided. Some felt that the Royal Duke, who was a great local benefactor, had every right to enclose his own land, but others were in favour of retaining the long-held right-of-way across The Warren. Funds were raised and the matter taken to the Law Courts. The trial opened in Croydon in 1853 by which time the Estate had been inherited by George, the second Duke.

The jury decided that the public did have pedestrian right-of-way, but that carriages should be restricted. Furthermore the costs of the case were to be met by the Duke who was so angry at the outcome of this affair that he refused to have anything to do with public life in Kingston for some considerable time afterwards.

The legacy of this court ruling applies today. Warren Road is a public footpath but special permits are still needed to drive a vehicle along the road.

For a hundred years there was a world-famous horticultural Nursery on the edge of the Warren near to Kingston Hill. It had been founded in 1856 by James Veitch on 35 acres of land leased from the Duke of Cambridge. The Veitch's - who also had nurseries in Chelsea and Exeter - were famous for acquiring rare and exotic plants from all over the world and successfully introducing them into British gardens.

Coombe Wood Nursery was renowned for the cultivation of rhododendrons, acers and water plants. On their Coombe site the Veitch's constructed a Japanese Water Garden, which was fed by the many springs for which the area was famous.

In 1915 the Nursery was sold to Arthur Luff and Sons - and it was to continue here until the 1950's, although some of the land had earlier been bought by the owners of Warren House. Much of the site has since been developed for housing but the beautiful Japanese Gardens still exist today, incorporated into the grounds of the new housing development along Warren Road. This is called, appropriately enough, 'The Water Gardens'.

The second Duke of Cambridge and great local benefactor being given the Freedom of the Borough in 1898 by the Mayor, Dr Finny.

This was in recognition of gift of the land upon which the Victoria Hospital had been built. (Later the Eye Hospital in Coombe Road, this building has now been redeveloped into apartments).

For almost over a thousand years, possibly longer, the lands of Coombe have been cultivated. The produce supplied the local Manor and it was also sold at the markets in Kingston and further afield. By 1837 there were three large tenanted farms on the Estate. (See also the Estate map on Page 4).

Hoppingwood Farm was where we now have Malden Golf Course, Cricket Club, Beverley Park and parts of New Malden. It was being worked from at least the early 1700's and the farmland was later bisected by the London to Southampton Railway Line when it opened in 1838. It was the first of the three farms to disappear when the land was sold for development in 1911.

Robin Hood Farm, which also dated from the early 1700's, was still being farmed until 1933, when part of the land was sold for housing. The rest was used to make way for the new A3 Kingston By-pass when it was opened in 1927, the first such road scheme to be built in the country.

Coombe Ridge House today stands on land which was part of Coombe Farm, once the busy and thriving Home Farm belonging to Coombe Manor House. In addition to the widespread fields and pastures this farm at one time consisted of numerous outhouses, including brewery, dairy, slaughterhouse and granaries.

During the 1640's a new farmhouse was built on Coombe Lane West by the owner of the Estate, Viscount Cullen. This original building was further enlarged in later years until it became a substantial residence in its own right. From hence onwards the farm was leased independently from the Manor House. Indeed from 1746 until 1912 only three different families were occupiers.

The Garner family, who were tenants during the first half of the 19th century, increased the acreage of the farm by cultivating further land on The Warren. (This part of the farm was described in the 1840 Tithe Map as 'rough pasture'; so presumably it was used to graze livestock).

By the latter half of the 19th century the farmlands began to decrease in size as the fields and pastures were gradually sold off for development. By the 1930's more of the acreage was sold for new housing. However a small farm was still operative up until the 1960's, centred on the 300 year-old farmhouse. Finally in 1968 this too disappeared and the farmhouse was demolished the following year. On its site today are Coombe Infants and Junior Schools.

Coombe Hill Farmhouse on Coombe Lane West before it was demolished in 1968.

Some of its land was developed in the late 1800's and the rest was sold for housing development in the 1930's, although a small-scale chicken and pig farm still existed here until 1968.

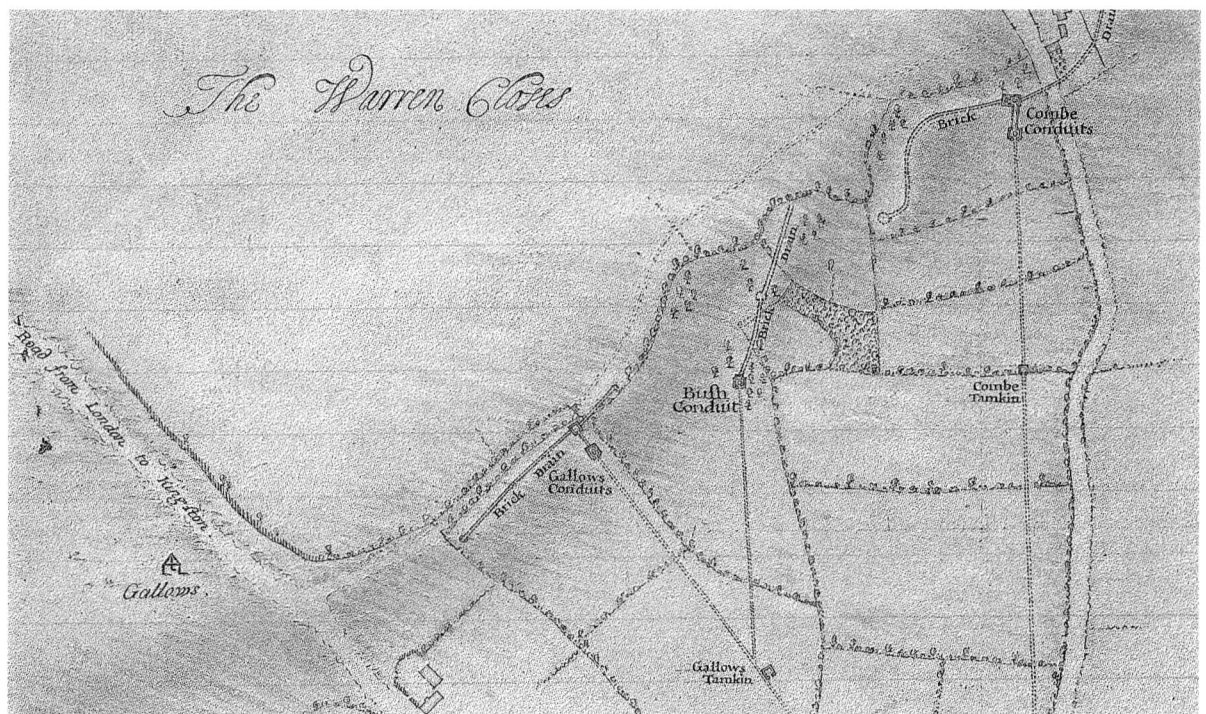

Part of an early map of the entire Conduit system, which also shows the fields of Coombe Farm around where Coombe Ridge House is today. Above the hedgerow at the top there is an ancient track which ran from the Fox and Coney on Kingston Hill to the left, to Coombe Farmhouse and Manor House top right.

The path, which was possibly then called London Lane, would have been a shortcut across the hill and was probably used by the 'Plombers'

(Plumbers) whose job it was to maintain the Conduit Houses for the Royal Palace at Hampton Court. It also shows a gallows site, on the top left, which may have been the Gallows upon which Blessed William Way was executed (See page 20) although this has never been fully substantiated.

This track which was one of several which ran across the hill, is not the George Road that we know today.

The track in fact no longer exists.

Hay-making, south of Coombe Lane West, c1920. These fields are now houses and gardens, which were built during and after the 1930's.

25

Old Coombe Estate Maps, dating from when Earl Spencer held the Estate in 1820 and which are today in The British Library, show that the Earl had intended to sell off around 50 acres of land on The Warren (now part of Coombe Hill and Coombe Wood golf courses) for what was presumably intended as an up-market housing estate.

There were to be at least nine plots for development, with several new roads across The Warren for access, although the gravel pits and some of the Warren and farmlands were to be retained.

This scheme was never carried out and by the time the Duke of Cambridge bought the Estate in 1837 Coombe was still a sparsely populated rural area, with only a few houses in the whole of the Estate.

Those few early residents who did need to travel to and from London would have had to make an uncomfortable road journey by private carriage or public stage-coach. However the opening of the 'Coombe-with-Malden' Railway Station in 1846 combined with improvements in the road systems meant that for the first time there were to be quicker and easier means of transport to the capital.

Consequently the increasing demand from the wealthy middle and upper classes for building land close to London meant that the now easily accessible Coombe Estate became a prime location.

By the 1860's the second Duke of Cambridge had decided to capitalise on his ownership of Coombe by selling off parcels of land, as had been the intention of the previous owner Earl Spencer.

A c1908 photograph of Coombe and Malden Railway Station.

By 1910 there were 56 trains daily to Waterloo and a first class return cost two shillings - ten pence today.

We have an account of what the area must have been like at this time from the author John Galsworthy's descriptions of 'Robin Hill', the fictional location in the 'Forsyte Saga', which he based on his childhood home of Coombe. In 'A Man of Property' the writer drew upon his own father's experiences of having been one of the first prospective buyers of the newly-available building land.

Just as John Galsworthy Senior must have done, the character Soames Forsyte travelled down by train from London, alighted at 'Robin Hill' Station (now New Malden) and walked up to the ridge of the hill on the edge of the ancient Warren.

Accompanied by his architect Bosinney, Soames viewed the plot of land he was proposing to buy. In the following extract Galsworthy described how the view from the top of 'Robin Hill' (Coombe Ridge) inspired the character to buy the land, as it had done his own father in 1865:

"They had struck into a half-made road across the warren. A cart track led at right angles to a gravel pit, beyond which the chimneys of a cottage rose amongst a clump of trees at the border of a thick wood. Tussocks of feathery grass covered the rough surface of the ground, and out of these the larks soared into the haze of sunshine....Almost from their feet stretched ripe corn, dipping to a small copse beyond. A plain of fields and hedges spread to the distant grey-blue downs.....In spite of himself, something swelled in his breast. To live here in sight of all this.....to talk of it, to possess it!"

Like the fictional Soames Forsyte John Galsworthy did indeed mean to possess the land with its magnificent views of the surrounding farmlands and distant Surrey Downs.

He took a 93 year lease from the Duke of Cambridge on 24-acres of land stretching down from the hill between what we know today as George Road/Coombe Lane West. It was here that he built 'Coombe Warren'; the first of the three houses that the family were to own on Coombe Hill.

"The architect was sprawling under a large oak tree, (which) .... stood on the verge of the rise ....

'.... this site will cost me half as much again'.(Soames).

'Hang the cost man. Look at the view!'"

(JG: 'A Man of Property').

John Galsworthy Senior came originally from Plymstock in Devon, where his father had been a merchant. Later the family had moved to London and founded what was to become an extremely successful property investment business. As well as working in the family concerns Mr Galsworthy became a successful solicitor and varied his activities by accepting directorships of companies involved in mining operations in Canada and Russia.

In business he was a man who commanded a great deal of respect. By speculation and shrewd management he had amassed a considerable personal fortune and at the age of 45 he decided to marry. He chose for his bride Blanche Bartleet, a woman some 20 years younger than himself, who came from a well-connected Worcestershire family.

In 1864 whilst living in Portland Place in London, their first child Lilian was born. Mr Galsworthy was determined that not only would his family have as many of the material comforts as possible, but that his children should enjoy all the benefits of growing up in a country environment, as he himself had done in Devon.

Therefore as soon as he had acquired his lease on the land on Coombe Hill and in order to supervise closely the work on the building of his new home, Mr Galsworthy moved his family temporarily to 'Parkfield', a rented house on Kingston Hill (now Galsworthy House). It was here that John, his eldest son, was born during a violent thunderstorm in 1867.

The following year the family moved into their fine new home, which they named Coombe Warren*. They were to live in this imposing Victorian-Gothic style house on the south facing ridge of the hill for the next seven years. In 1869, another son, Hubert, was born and the last child Mabel Edith arrived in 1871.

(* Coombe Warren and its grounds occupied a site which is now The Drive and Orchard Rise).

John Galsworthy (1817-1904) and his wife Blanche Galsworthy (1837-1915) the parents of John, the author.

They were amongst the first of the property developers to come to Coombe in the mid to late 1800's and build houses here.

Coombe Warren, the Galsworthy's first house, was not long to remain the only property on the ridge of the hill as in 1873 another house was built on the pasture-land next door. Then called 'South Warren', it was later to be known as Coombe Leigh and then finally Coombe Ridge House.

The first resident, William Dunville, was a wealthy solicitor, originally from County Down in Ireland, who lived there with his wife Anne. We can assume that South Warren was to be their 'country home' as they owned several other properties including a house in London. Sadly they were not long to enjoy their Coombe home because a year after they moved in William Dunville died. As the couple did not have any children the bulk of his considerable estate was inherited by his widow Anne and for some reason she soon decided to sell 'South Warren'.

By this time the property was some eight acres in total and included 'Messuage or tenement, coach-house, stables and other buildings'. It was bought for £6,000 by her neighbour John Galsworthy and in 1875 his family moved in.

Today we have no definite proof or documentation to indicate who actually built Coombe Ridge House. According to William Dunville's will, he had sub-leased four acres of land from John Galsworthy in 1873 and at the same time leased around two further acres from the Duke of Cambridge. What is not clear is whether the four acres of land leased from Galsworthy also included a house, or if Dunville subsequently had one constructed one on the site.

The balance of probability is that Galsworthy did build a house here and immediately afterwards sold it to the Dunvilles. This would have been in keeping with his usual practice of buying land, building on it and then selling it for profit. Galsworthy, as we know, was a highly successful property developer.

Further evidence to support this theory comes from the Galsworthy children's recollections, in which they stated that their father had built all three of their Coombe homes. In conclusion therefore, although it is not clear who built the house, what is apparent is that the Galsworthy family were not the first occupants of Coombe Ridge House as has always been assumed.

Rare photograph c1874 which shows the Galsworthy family's FIRST home Coombe Warren (now demolished). In the background can be seen the outline and rooftops of Coombe Ridge House (then called South Warren) when it was the home of William and Anne Dunville.

Coombe Warren was sold to Daniel Watney in 1875 and the gardens were later beautifully landscaped by him.

The four Galsworthy children who all had such happy memories of living in Coombe.

Lilian	John
Hubert	Mabel

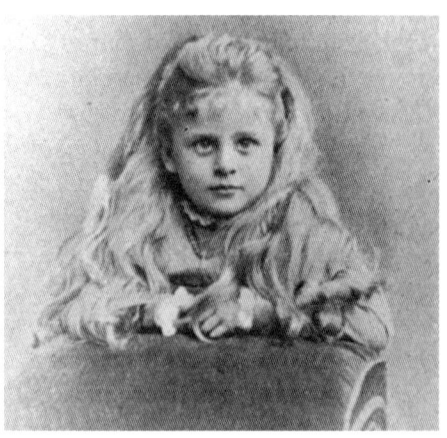

When they bought 'South Warren' the Galsworthy family renamed the house 'Coombe Leigh', or as they were to simply call it 'The Leigh'. This house was to be the favourite home of the Galsworthy children and they lived here twice from 1875-1878 and from 1881 until 1886. In between they lived at their third house on George Road 'Coombe Croft', today home to Rokeby School.

By the time that they first moved in, during September 1875, the household consisted of the parents, John and Blanche and their four young children aged 11, 9, 6 and 3. To see to their needs there was also a large staff of eight 'indoor' and six 'outdoor' servants. The staff lived upstairs in the attics, in the gatekeeper's lodge and in the stable cottage. When the family had large dinner parties, extra staff were also drafted in to help!

The family had at least four carriages which were housed in the large coach-house, as well as a small T-cart which their coachman 'portly old Haddon' taught them to drive. They would often accompany him as he drove their father to and from Coombe & Malden station. Sometimes Haddon supervised them when they rode their ponies in nearby Richmond Park.

On Sundays the family travelled to St John the Baptist Church at nearby Kingston Vale, where John Galsworthy was a Vicar's Warden.

The household was fairly self-sufficient, as there were extensive kitchen gardens and glass-houses for growing fruit and vegetables and a small home farm which housed pigs, chickens and cows. There were also orchards and a horse paddock. Other supplies were delivered by Mr Sawdy the local grocer, although their tea came directly from India where Blanche's brother had a tea plantation.

As was usual in wealthy Victorian households, the Galsworthy children saw very little of their mother, who was more of a distant figure in their lives. It was said that when they lived in Coombe, she was often unwell and spent much of her time at 'The Leigh' reclining on the sofa in the Drawing Room.

However (and unusually for the time) they spent a great deal of time with their father, who delighted in the company of his small children. He had, it was said, infinite patience with them.

His working day was apparently not overlong. He would leave home at 11am to travel by train up to his office in the City of London, returning home at 5 pm in the afternoon, which gave him plenty of time to enjoy his country home! In the evening he would tour his garden in the company of his children who took great delight in inspecting the farm animals and the wildlife with their beloved father.

Above: Coombe Road, as it looked c1900.

This is part of the route that the Galsworthy children took when they went to meet their father from the station.

John Galsworthy Senior was the role model for 'Old Jolyon' in 'The Forsyte Saga'.

Left is a photo from the BBC production and shows Joseph O'Connor (Jolyon) and Jackie Smith (Holly) in the grounds of the fictitious 'Robin Hill'.

Galsworthy's childhood home was the inspiration for the setting of the Forsyte's house.

Life at 'The Leigh'

We are fortunate today that we have some detailed and evocative accounts of the young Galsworthy childhoods, taken from both John and Mabel's later recollections.

When they were little the children spent most of their time upstairs in the nursery and schoolroom, where they were looked after by their beloved nursery maid, Bella Spraggins. Their lessons were taught by a series of French and English governesses. As they grew older, the girls continued their education at home but the two boys were sent away to boarding school, firstly attending a small preparatory school in Bournemouth and later going to Harrow.

The children were rarely allowed in any of the grander rooms on the ground floor but were sometimes permitted to play in the Billiards Room. Mabel recalled that she used to chalk up the scores for her two brothers and from where she sat she could see out onto the beautiful rose-garden at the side of the house.

When they tired of playing inside, the children would run through the French doors which led into the big glass conservatory, down the steps to the terrace and then out onto to the lawns. Here the boys played tennis, watched by Mabel from the swing in the big old oak tree. Sometimes the boys climbed up this tree and fired pea shooters and water pistols at the long-suffering gardeners.

John and Hubert loved to play cricket and once when a friend from school visited he thought that the family must have been very wealthy, as they had their own pitch to practice on. On long summer days the young John entertained himself and his brother and sisters by making up imaginative and exciting games and in quieter moments Lilian, the eldest child, would tell them wonderful stories.

They took delight in helping the servants with the chores, offering to collect fruit from the greenhouses, kitchen gardens or orchard. Sometimes they would collect eggs from the chicken coop or fresh milk from their own Alderney cow. A further treat was to assist the coachman and groom with the horses and ponies in the stables.

From all their accounts it appears that they had an idyllic childhood in all three of their Coombe homes and many happy memories of 'The Leigh'.

The house and grounds of Coombe Ridge House

Billiard Room

Rose Garden

Conservatory

Drawing Room

Kitchen and staff area
(Ground floor)

Nursery wing
(First Floor)

Stable block

The greenhouses

The little farm

Orchard

"**T**he moment he was suffered to get up, he rigged his bed fore and aft, and set out from it in a narrow bath across seas of green carpet, to a rock, which he climbed by means of its mahogany drawer knobs, to sweep the horizon with his drinking tumbler screwed to his eye, in search of rescuing sails."

Extract from the book called 'Awakening', in 'the Forsyte Saga', in which young Jon Forsyte is creating his own imaginary world of pirates, ships and adventure, using anything he had to hand in the nursery, just as John Galsworthy and his brother and sisters did in Coombe.

Apparently the games sometimes became quite heated as the boys resorted to pillow fights and no doubt later tellings-off from their nurse!

In 1924, John Galsworthy published privately a short essay entitled 'Memorable Days'. In this rare piece - only 60 copies were ever published - we have a small boy's eyewitness account of the events leading up to the lavish dinner parties which his parents frequently gave in their Coombe homes. It was written about the period when the family were living at 'The Leigh'.

John Galsworthy as a boy. He evidently had very many happy memories of his childhood in Coombe. From this story it is apparent that even at a very early age he observed in minute detail the things that went on around him.

"These were the days when my Father's house was full of preparations for a dinner party, and I would be hard at work during all the hours not given up to lessons. First, I had to attend the head gardener in the hothouse and the vinery, selecting the pineapples and grapes; or from the south wall picking the peaches and nectarines; nor could I on any account be absent when Henry the butler, with two wicker baskets, and my Father, opened the door which kept in that half-nice, funny smell, as of gas and mushrooms.

With my hands in my waist belt, and my legs apart, I would stare up at my father handling the bottles with extreme care, and with his thin, taper-nailed fingers holding them up to the light. And I used to pretend that I was in a dungeon, and be very careful to be in front when we brought the bottles up. I had also constantly to see exactly what was eaten, and be told; 'Now Master Johnny, don't touch!"

....

"All this would be in the morning. The afternoon would be even more exciting for quite early, my friend Mr Sawdy the greengrocer, who had whiskers and such a pale nice face, and was pleased with my society, and my friend Glover, who could wink, would arrive, beautifully dressed, with white gloves in their pockets (Because I saw them) to help Henry and Francois put the extra leaves in the Dining table, and lay it and the sideboard. Every time I came in to see, the room would look more and more snowy, and smell nicer and nicer of melon and pineapple and flowers; till at last I would say to Mr Sawdy: 'I might have a wafer now Mr Sawdy'. And Mr Sawdy would look round......"

"I was not so interested in the flowers, which my mother would be arranging in the library, and bringing in. I liked the smell, and the colours, but I felt that they were not serious like the melon, or the peaches, or the wafers. Nor was I interested in the drawing rooms on these days, because there was nothing there that was going to be eaten, they just looked all shiny and had no-one in there yet. Sometimes all the twenty people, except my Father and Mother, would be coming specially - some of them all the way from London - in their carriages; but sometimes there would be guests staying in the house, especially my Uncle Wally and my cousin Evie".

"I had to go and hear my Father say to Mother: 'Now Blanche, you'll be late'. But I had to stand in the doorway, so that my Father could not go without wrestling with me, this he would do very seriously, puffing a little to show me how strong I was then suddenly slide me between his legs and leave me on the floor".

....

"I could hear the carriages driving up, and see Henry walking across the hall with a lady and gentleman behind him, and hear him say: 'General and Mrs Grim'* and then he would stand still at the drawing room door while they all came up and blew in his ear, one after the other, and he would say like this:' Mr and Lady Evelyn Tushby*, Sir Edgar and Lady Dulane and Miss Dulane* ahem!' This lasted a long time and there was such a nice loud noise of talking, which made me feel buzzy and excited. Then Henry shut the door and it was quiet".

"I knew then that they had all come, and that was some how nice. I could see Henry standing alone down there, and once I saw him put his thumb up to his nose and spread out his fingers and point them at the door. But before I could say 'Henry' and ask him why, he opened the Dining Room Door and went in. He always came out very quickly, and opened the Drawing Room door and said: 'Dinner is served'.".

(* The names of the guests John Galsworthy referred to are people who lived locally, but he has changed the names slightly. General Grim was Colonel Sim at Coombe House; the Tushby's were the Bushby's, who lived at Henleigh on Kingston Hill and the Dulane's were Sir Edmund and Lady Mary Du Cane from Coombe Springs).

(Extracted from Memorable Days, by John Galsworthy. Curwen Press 1924).

The Galsworthy family when they were on holiday in Scotland.

This photograph was taken shortly before the family left Coombe for good in 1886. They returned to live in London as the children were by now grown up.

In 1904, old John Galsworthy died. His wife Blanche (not shown here) was to survive him until 1915.

Coombe Leigh was bought from the Galsworthy's for £12,000 in 1886 by William Middleton Campbell and it was then that the name was changed to Coombe Ridge House.

William Campbell was born in Scotland in 1849, where his family were descended from a long line of Scottish land-owners. He joined the family business (they were sugar merchants who had made a fortune by trading in the West Indies) and later he became a Deputy Lieutenant of Dunbartonshire.

William Middleton Campbell (1849-1919).

A Director and later Governor of the Bank of England, he lived in Coombe Ridge House with his family from 1886 until 1898.

From his portrait and the later recollections of his descendants, William Middleton Campbell appears to have been an authoritarian and forthright character.

On one occasion, some distant relations asked if they could stay the night whilst travelling nearby. WMC, who did not like the couple, instructed his wife to put them off. When she demurred, William said that he would do it himself. He sent a terse telegram which simply said:

'Prefer you not to come Tuesday'!

At some stage in his career Mr Campbell moved south to London, presumably to look after the family's business concerns in the City. In the same year that he moved into Coombe Ridge House he became a Director of the Bank of England and later he held the important and influential post of Governor from 1907 until 1909.

The banking connection is evidently very strong in the family, as in 1873 he had married Edith Agneta Bevan, daughter of the millionaire Banker Robert Cooper Lee Bevan. When they arrived in Coombe the Campbells already had four children: Colin, Agneta, Ronald and Norman, aged 12, 9, 8 and 6 respectively. The following year another boy, Evan was born in the house.

Once again Coombe Ridge House was full of young children and no doubt their cousins, who lived next door also came to play. From around 1890 until 1899 Coombe Court was home to Edith's brother Wildfred Bevan, his wife Mary and their six daughters.

Three of the boys in the family were sent to be educated at Eton and later Trinity College, Cambridge. The daughter, Agneta, was married from Coombe Ridge House in 1898. Her husband was Sir Alfred Ernest Tritton, Bt, who was the son of the MP for Lambeth. (The two families had strong business associations through the long-established Barclay, Bevan and Tritton Banking Partnership. This subsequently became Barclays Bank under the Chairmanship of yet another Bevan brother, Frances).

The Campbell family left the area in 1899 when they moved to Sussex, and for the third time, Coombe Ridge House was up for sale.....

There was great excitement in the house when the Campbell's only daughter was married in All Saints Church, Kingston, on June 22nd 1898. The wedding was attended by hundreds of wealthy and important guests and the proceedings were reported at great length in 'The Surrey Comet'. The following is a short extract of what was described in the paper as: 'The Marriage of the Season'.

'Considerable interest was manifested in the event and a large and fashionable congregation were present in the church to witness the nuptials, the costumes and toilets being in many instances exceedingly handsome'.

'The event was favoured by ideal summer weather, the scene being gladdened by a brilliant flood of golden sunshine, which shone without intermission, and considerably enhanced the happiness of the occasion.'

'Mr and Mrs Middleton Campbell subsequently held the reception at Coombe Ridge House, the proceedings being enlivened by some excellent music furnished by the Royal Artillery Band. Dejeurner was served in a marquee on the lawn.....A large number of carriages were required to convey the bridal party and guests to and from the church, and the arrival and departure were witnessed by a large concourse of spectators'.

'The Wedding of the Season'. The Wedding Reception for Sir Alfred and Lady Agneta Tritton, as it would have looked in the grounds of Coombe Ridge House on that long-ago summer afternoon in 1898.

37

By the time the Campbell family left the area at the end of the nineteenth century Coombe had become established as one of the most fashionable and desirable places in which to live. The fine views, excellent air quality and the relatively close proximity to London meant that many of the leading members of high society had also decided to make Coombe their home.

Map which shows the Coombe Mansion Houses c1900. (S e e s c h e d u l e opposite and overleaf for details). This period in history was when Coombe was the epicentre of high society.

Several of the imposing mansion houses that were built here played host to many important visitors including members of the British and other Royal families, Cabinet ministers and politicians, as well as stars from the opera and ballet. It could be said that during the hey-day of Edwardian high-society, anyone who was anyone was either a Coombe resident or listed amongst the guests. Amongst the 'entertainments' offered was the shooting of game and according to the 1910 'Borough Pocket Guidebook', Coombe Woods were said to be still providing ample 'bags' of pheasant.

Therefore, we will take just a brief look at some of the other big houses that were built on the Coombe Estate by the turn of the century and what has happened to them since then.....

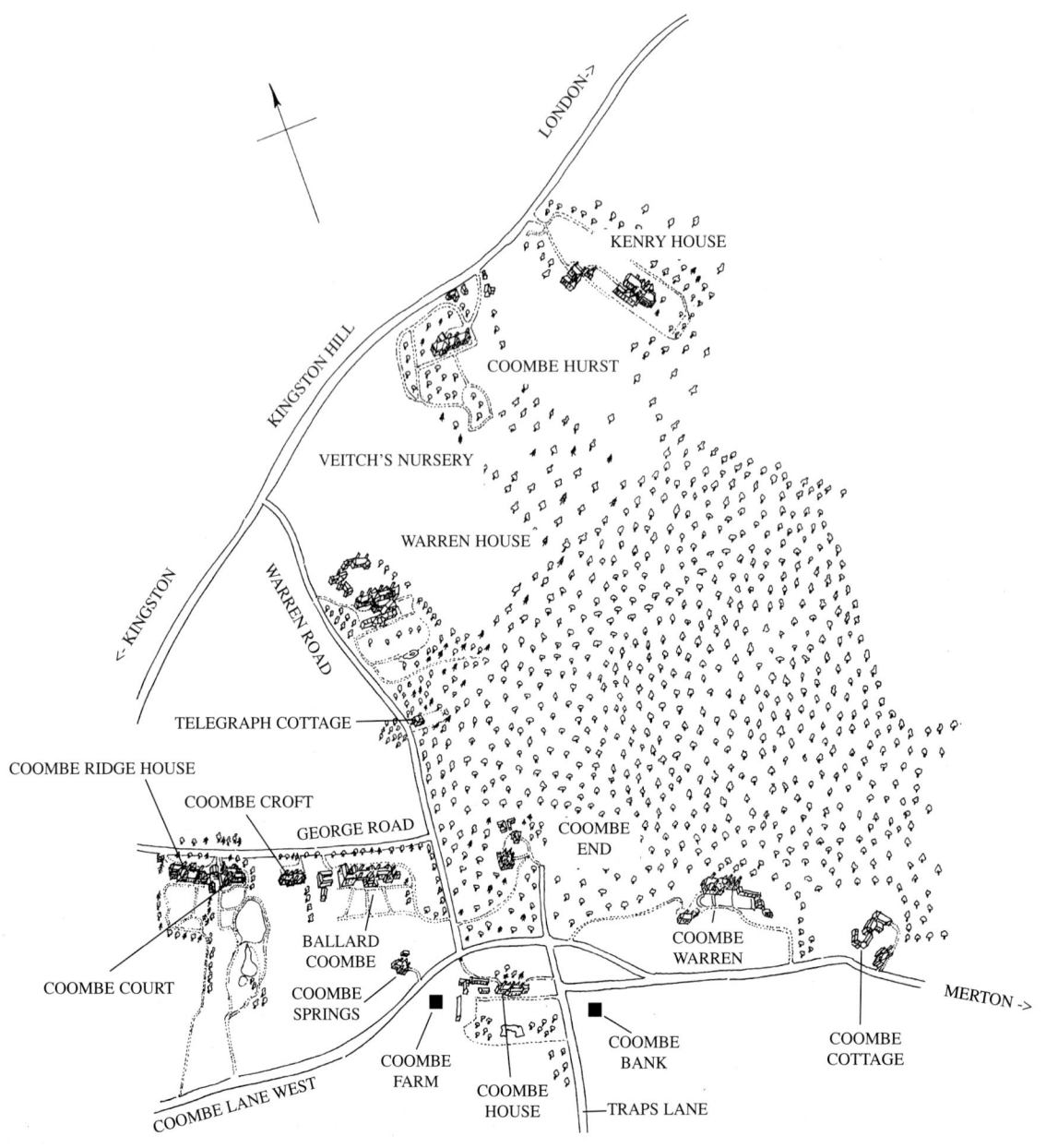

1.   Kenry House, built in 1832, one of the first houses to be built in Coombe and originally known as Coombe Wood. From 1874-1926 it was home to the diligent Earl of Dunraven, (Baron Kenry). During his life he was a war correspondent, hunted with Buffalo Bill, bred and trained horses, was a master mariner and yachtsman. He commanded his own steam yacht as a hospital ship during the First World War and was also involved in Irish politics. Kenry House is now owned by Kingston University.

2.   Coombe Hurst, built in 1835 by Samuel Smith, Uncle to Florence Nightingale. She was a frequent visitor here as a child. From 1885-1915 it was home to Captain de Grey Vyner, a wealthy racehorse and stud-farm owner and brother-in-law of the Marquis of Ripon (See Coombe Court). Now also now part of Kingston University.

3.   Warren House, built in 1865 by Hugh Hammersley. In 1884 it was bought by George Grenfell Glyn, 2nd Baron Wolverton, a Banker who was a close associate of Bertram W Currie (See Coombe Warren) and Edward Baring (See Coombe Cottage).He was also a friend of W Gladstone, the Prime Minister, who was a frequent visitor here, as were members of the British Royal Family. This was one of the last buildings worked on by George Devey, the renowned architect, who made several alterations to the house. At the turn of the century it was home to a G. Cawston and then for nearly 50 years, until 1954, it was home to Sir Arthur and Dame Leila Paget. This house is today the ICI Training Centre, although some of its grounds were sold for redevelopment.

4.   Coombe Ridge House, formerly Coombe Leigh, built in 1873. Home to the Galsworthy's and several other prominent families. Now Holy Cross Preparatory School.

5.   Coombe Court, formerly Coombe Warren, built in 1868 by John Galsworthy Senior, sold to Daniel Watney, who designed the magnificent landscaped gardens. Then home to a Banker, Wilfred Bevan and in 1899 to Earl de Grey, later Marquis of Ripon and his beautiful wife Gladys. They extended the house and it became famous for the elegant high-society parties that were held here. It was inherited by Gladys' daughter Lady Juliet Duff, who continued to entertain here on a vast scale for many years. The house was demolished and the grounds were sold for development in 1931. The houses in The Drive occupy the site.

5. Coombe Court

6.   Coombe Croft, the third and smallest of the Galsworthy houses, built in 1878. It was then the home to the Norton family for many years, who were still resident in 1900. It later became Gate House School and is now Rokeby Preparatory School.

6.   Coombe Croft, when it was Gate House School.

7.   Ballard Coombe, Originally built c1890 it was at the turn of the century home to Kenelm Lee Guinness, the motor racing driver and inventor, who at one time held the world land speed record. Later home to the Earl of Listowel, the house was rebuilt in 1927 following a fire. It is now Marymount International School.

8. Coombe Springs

8.   Coombe Springs, built in 1840, it was home to Sir Edmund and Lady Du Cane and at the turn of the century it was owned by Sir Douglas Fox. It was later bought by Mr and Mrs Hwfa Williams who founded Sandown Race-course at Esher. Florence Williams was a renowned society hostess and many distinguished guests visited here. The house has now been demolished.

11. Coombe Warren

9.   Coombe End, up until the turn of the century it was the home of the Earl of Tankerville, with 17 bed and dressing rooms set in 21 acres of land.

Now new housing here which is also called 'Coombe End'.

10.   Coombe House, one-time Manor House to the Estate, it was rebuilt in the 1750's by Earl Spencer and was later home to Lord Liverpool. (See Pages 16-19). Coombe House was demolished in 1933 and on its site are the new houses around Coombe House Chase and Fitzgeorge/Neville Avenues.

11.   Coombe Warren, built in 1861 and rebuilt after a fire in 1870 by Bertram Wodehouse Currie. (He was a great friend of Prime Minister Gladstone, who was a frequent visitor and once held Cabinet here when he was recuperating from an illness). The architect for this lavishly-decorated house, with its magnificent landscaped gardens was again George Devey and the house was considered by many to be one of his finest works. Coombe Warren was lived in by the Currie family until 1926, when it was amongst the first of the mansion houses to be demolished, although some of the estate cottages survive as private residences. The area where it stood is around Coombe Hill Road/Beverley Lane.

12.   Coombe Cottage, was bought in 1863 by the banker Edward Baring (later Lord Revelstoke) who was the great-great grandfather of Diana, Princess of Wales. He subsequently employed Devey to extend this house into an enormous 60-roomed mansion.

A guest for a time in 1881 was the widow of Napoleon III, Empress Eugenie and later still Coombe Cottage was home to the world-famous operatic diva, Dame Nellie Melba. When she returned to Australia, she called her house there 'Coombe Cottage'. The original Coombe Cottage has now been developed into luxury apartments.

When the house was sold for £9,000 in 1899 it was bought by two brothers, Harold and Arthur Tangye. They were sons of Sir Richard Tangye, a world-famous businessman and engineer. For several months they leased the house to a Mr G Hughes and then from 1901-1903 their parents lived in Coombe Ridge House.

Richard Tangye was originally from Cornwall, where his father had been a farmer and shopkeeper and by the age of eight he was already helping out by working on the family farm. From these humble beginnings he went on to train as an engineer in Birmingham and later, with his three brothers, established what was to become a highly successful machine manufacturing company in the Midlands, which was internationally renowned for its innovation.

In 1856 the Tangye brothers supplied Brunel with the hydraulic lifts that were instrumental in the successful launch of his famous steamship. Sir Richard was to later say of this event, "We launched the Great Eastern, and She launched us!" The Tangye Company went from strength to strength and in 1878 their lifts were used to help site Cleopatra's Needle on the Thames Embankment. The brothers were pioneers in establishing fair working conditions for their employees, well in advance of their day and were later to become generous benefactors to the City of Birmingham.

Sir Richard and his wife Caroline had come to Coombe to retire. Although often in ill-health he participated actively in Kingston's social and political affairs and at one time presented the prizes at Tiffin Boys School.

In 1903 Sir Richard and Lady Tangye left Coombe Ridge House to move to another large house nearby, Coombe Bank (now demolished). It was here that Sir Richard fell ill in 1906 and for several days in October of that year the Court News in 'The Times' carried details of his deteriorating health. He died later in the month and was buried in Putney Vale Cemetery; his funeral attended by hundreds of mourners.

In the days when world-wide travel was often difficult, if not dangerous, Sir Richard travelled seven times to Australia and twice to New Zealand. He also liked to write and in 1897 he contributed to the Kingston Vale Parish Magazine an article entitled 'The Greatness of Little Things', which was a little homily intended presumably for the young people of the parish of St John the Baptist. It is worth mentioning here, if only for its insight into the character of Sir Richard, who apparently he did not like to waste time. His closing remarks in the essay were:

"And so to sum up the whole matter I would say, Whatsoever thy hand findeth to do, do it with all thy might, and DO IT AT ONCE!"

Sir Richard Tangye, 1833-1906, the world-famous engineer and businessman, who lived in Coombe Ridge House for two years.

41

In 1903 the house was again sold, this time for £7,750, to the Reverend William Ewart Beamish Barter and his wife Mary Constance and their children. The Reverend Barter was by then Minister of Grosvenor Chapel in South Audley Street, London. This was a chapel-at-ease to St George's Hanover Square; a parish in which he served and was associated with for many years.

weekend parties, which were attended by the cream of high society.

Their guests included His Royal Highness, King Edward VIIth and Queen Alexandra ,as well as members of other European Royal families.

As dusk fell, the Ripon servants would have lit the hundreds of lanterns which illuminated the

A picturesque photograph which shows the view from the terrace of Coombe Court, next door to Coombe Ridge House.

These wonderful Italian gardens were the scene of so many high-society parties before and after the First World War.

From the St.George's Church records we know that he was Editor of the Parish Magazine and was in charge of the Working Men's Club, the Gymnasium and Bible classes. He also ran the Temperance Society, which was an organisation which strongly disapproved of imbibing alcohol and other 'vices'.

In view of the fact that the Reverend strongly promoted sobriety and restraint, we can only surmise what he must have thought of the 'Goings-on' next door which must have been clearly visible from the upper windows of Coombe Ridge House.

By then his neighbours at Coombe Court were the Marquis and Marchioness of Ripon. The couple were renowned for their sumptuous

grounds. Inside the sumptuous new ballroom, which had been built for Gladys, the Marchioness, the guests were entertained by such celebrities as the opera singers Dame Nellie Melba and Caruso, as well as the leading stars of the Russian Ballet Company.

The evocative sounds of beautiful music, merry laughter and champagne corks popping would have been clearly heard by Reverend Barter. We can imagine that he would have looked on with disapproval at all this high-spirited and probably most intemperate behaviour so close to home!

Reverend Barter was to remain at Coombe Ridge House until 1920, by which time the property was once again up for sale.

The Reverend Barter was, we know, a very keen and talented golfer who played 'off scratch' and was one of the original members of Coombe Wood Golf Course next door and opposite his house.

(The Club, which was then only a 9 hole course had been opened in 1904 by the Prime Minister, A J Balfour).

Revd. Barter was still playing up until 1919, when he represented the Coombe Wood Club in a match against Raynes Park. From the club records it was stated that the Reverend looked most impressive and the Club won the match.

Below is an artist's impression of our golf-playing Reverend, as he played on the Coombe Wood Golf Course. In the background can be seen the rooftops of Coombe Ridge House.

The golf-playing Reverend William Beamish Barter, Owner of Coombe Ridge House and one of the earliest members of Coombe Wood Golf Club.

In 1919 Coombe Ridge House was put up for Auction and we have obtained a copy of the Sale Brochure from this time. This is the first page which describes what accommodation was available then.

By the standards of the other large houses around Coombe Ridge House was considered to be relatively modest, but note how many bed and dressing rooms there were!

KINGSTON HILL

ON THE COOMBE ESTATE, ONE MILE FROM NORBITON STATION.

PARTICULARS, PLAN, VIEWS AND
CONDITIONS OF SALE

OF THE

Charming Family Residence

KNOWN AS

"COOMBE RIDGE"

beautifully situate on the FITZ-GEORGE ESTATE, away from all noise, and immediately overlooking the COOMBE WOOD GOLF LINKS. It comprises:

A HANDSOME RED-BRICK RESIDENCE

containing LOUNGE HALL, THREE FINE RECEPTION ROOMS, FULL-SIZED
BILLIARD ROOM, FOURTEEN BED AND DRESSING ROOMS,
THREE BATH ROOMS, and excellent Ground Floor Offices .

Stabling for 9 Horses

Large GARAGE, COACH-HOUSE, COTTAGE and LODGE

Beautiful Pleasure Grounds and Gardens, with Paddock,

The whole comprising an area of upwards of

8 Acres.

MAIN DRAINAGE and the COMPANY'S WATER.

———

For Sale by Auction (WITH POSSESSION) by Messrs.

COCKETT & HENDERSON

At WINCHESTER HOUSE, OLD BROAD STREET, E.C.
On TUESDAY, NOVEMBER 18th, 1919,
At 2.30 o'clock precisely.

Copies of these Particulars may be had of Messrs. CRUMP, SPROTT & CO., Solicitors, 13, Old Queen Street,
Westminster, S.W. 1 : and of the Auctioneers at their Offices, 100, Jermyn Street, S.W. 1.

By the end of the First World War, when millions of people were killed or injured, Britain was beginning to see the demise of the rigid class system.

Many of the soldiers who returned had different aspirations. The roles of women too were to be transformed, as other employment opportunities became available to them for the first time.

One of the effects of the War was that it became increasingly difficult to get domestic staff and it was from around this time that we start to see the decline of 'The Great Houses'. The fluctuating post-war financial circumstances of some landowners also meant that they were either unable to maintain, or forced to sell their land and estates. This national situation was reflected in Coombe and many of its large houses and estates were either in decline or changed hands during the post-War years. Amongst them was Coombe Ridge House.

In 1919 John Galsworthy made a nostalgic visit to his childhood home with his wife Ada, when the house was up for auction. He was apparently dismayed at the condition in which he found the house, as Ada was to later describe in her notebook:

"One Sunday we motored down to Coombe, and had a look over Coombe Leigh where J's family lived from 1875 to 1886, a hideously destroyed house, worse decorated and furnished than anything ever seen, and only the view unspoilt".

It seems a shame that John Galsworthy's happy memories should have been spoilt and as far as we know, the author never again returned.

In 1920 the house was bought for £7,500 by a Major James Platt and his wife Elsie.

Major Platt was we believe a horse trainer, as he wrote a book entitled: 'The Thoroughbred Racehorse', but his whereabouts during the First World War and after the Platt's left the house remain a mystery.

They lived in Coombe Ridge House with another couple until 1922 and then once again the house was for sale.

Two photographs of the house, taken from the 1919 Auction Brochure. If one looks carefully, it is just possible to make out the Conservatory on the back view of the house (far left).

At the front the entrance porch was different, and the hallway ran from the front to the back of the house.

It is interesting also to see how much ivy covered the building then.

The house was bought by Sir Frederick William Pascoe Rutter; Chairman, General Manager and subsequently Governor of the London and Lancashire Insurance Company Limited, now part of the Royal Insurance Group. He paid £7,500 for the property and around this time he also purchased the Freehold on the land itself. (He paid £4,250 to the owners of the land, the Fitzgeorges, who were heirs to the late Duke of Cambridge. In the following few years, the Fitzgeorge family were to sell the majority of their freehold land in Coombe).

Frederick Rutter had moved to Coombe with his wife Agnes from their London home. He had been born in Liverpool in 1859, and at the age of 14 began what was to be a 60-year successful and profitable working life in the insurance industry and in fact one of his contemporaries was to later describe him as being: 'One of the last Insurance tycoons in the world'.

When he first came to Coombe, and although by then in his sixties, he was still actively involved in 'The London and Lancashire'. The Company was his life and through his acquisition of other companies and his extensive travelling to establish agencies throughout the world he built it up to become one of the leading insurance companies in the country - and contributed to giving British insurance its world-leading position. As an employer, Frederick Rutter was said to have demanded high standards and was often hard on his managers, although it is said that he was held in great esteem by his junior staff - for whom he later gave garden parties at Coombe Ridge House.

In the course of his hard-working efforts, he had also shared in his company's prosperity and by the time he moved to Coombe he was a wealthy man. In the 27 years that he lived in the house he was to fill it with the many treasures he had collected from his numerous overseas trips.

Sir Frederick Pascoe Rutter, in the library of Coombe Ridge House, with Lord Hewart, who was Lord Chief Justice of England from 1922-1940.

It was in this very room that on October 14th 1933, Colonel Sir Augustus Fitzgeorge, the last surviving son of the Duke of Cambridge, fell ill whilst playing cards. He lost consciousness and went into a coma from which he never recovered.

Before they moved in to the house, the Rutters made several alterations to the building and such was the standard of the workmanship at the time that today it takes an expert eye to discern what is original and what are later additions.

All the windows in the 'family' part of the house were replaced with leaded glass, although the ones at the 'working' end of the house in the kitchens and servants' quarters were not replaced and are still today Victorian sash. The rooms downstairs and on the first floor were remodelled: some walls were removed and others added. The old entrance and hallway were altered and the porch moved. We think that the staircase too was altered at this time as the front wall was also moved several feet, possibly to create a lighter hallway. A 'new' library was created using part of the old hallway and new bookcases were installed.

Outside, the old glass conservatory was cleared away and the loggia (the covered area on the terrace) was built. The garden too was restored to its former glory with new flowerbeds and a rose trellis on the second terrace. This garden was to be the venue for some magnificent parties...

Frederick Pascoe Rutter 'at home' on the terrace of Coombe Ridge House with his grand-daughter Angela taken in the 1930's.

Behind them is the 'new' loggia that had been built when he bought the house, one of many alterations that he made.

For many years, the gardens of Coombe Ridge House were used as the venue for well-attended garden parties, held to entertain the staff of the London and Lancashire Insurance Company and also on behalf of the 'Lest We Forget' Association, an organisation which helped disabled War Veterans. During the 1920's and 1930's many ex-servicemen and their volunteer attendants were welcomed by the Rutters.

Frederick Pascoe Rutter in the grounds of his house, as reported in the 'Surrey Comet'.

One such memorable occasion was in 1933, when a 3-day party was held in the grounds and house. It was to celebrate both Frederick Pascoe Rutter's 60 years in insurance and to welcome the old soldiers. The event was reported at great length in the Surrey Comet at the time:

Another view of the memorable Garden Parties held in Coombe Ridge House before the Second World War.

"About 100 men were ..guests, and although many of them were chair cases, which meant that they were unable to move about, there were also a good number who were sufficiently active to be able to join in the games and competitions which had been organised and to wander around the lovely gardens of Coombe Ridge.... the chair cases were seated in the corner, form a natural stage... the orchestra played throughout the afternoon. Tea was served in a large marquee on the other side of the lawn and those men who could not be moved had theirs under the trees".

There was also a reference to the Ivy Conduit House, which at the time was undamaged:

"Mr Pascoe Rutter spent most of the afternoon and evening chatting with the men, and to several he showed the famous Ivy Conduit....Indeed, the well-house, with its thick walls and the ice-cold water with which the well is full to the brim, must have been quite one of the coolest places in Kingston that afternoon".

If only someone had thought to take a photograph of this event, then perhaps today we would have some idea of what it once looked like!

Mrs Rutter sadly died in 1929 and a Church Hall at St John the Baptist, Kingston Vale, was later dedicated in her honour. Frederick Rutter was created a Knight in 1934 and he continued to live in Coombe until his old age, including right through the Second World War.

Aerial reconnaisance photographs taken at the time show that much of his garden was used to grow vegetables and we know that the metal railings in the front garden were cut down and given to the War Effort. The house itself had some damage (today there are still schrapnel marks on some of the outside walls and Ivy Conduit House in the grounds was damaged by a V1 bomb which fell on the lawn nearby in 1944) yet in comparison with the rest of the country Coombe Ridge House and its occupants survived the War relatively unscathed.

The surrounding area was harder-hit. Some 90 residents of Malden and Coombe were killed and hundreds more injured. It was also estimated that practically every building in the area had some degree of damage and in one devastating daylight raid in 1940 over 80 local houses were destroyed.

It may seem surprising that a relatively rural area such as Coombe and Malden should have had so much damage during the War. One explanation for this (apart from the fact that the area is reasonably close to Kingston's aircraft factory and power station) is that during the War there was a secret military 'decoy town' set up near the Penn Ponds in nearby Richmond Park.

This was a system of incendiary devices which were set off as enemy bombers approached, designed to simulate the burning of previously bombed industrial sites and thus draw the enemy bombers away from authentic targets. Its existence and whereabouts may or may not have been known by the staff of one of Sir Frederick's wartime 'neighbours' across the golf course General Eisenhower.

The General wanted to find a 'country cottage' away from the bombing of Central London, which was also within easy travelling distance of the SHAEF* Headquarters in Bushey Park, just over the Thames River. (*Supreme Headquarters Allied Expiditionary Force; the combined allied military operation).

General Eisenhower lived in Coombe for some months in 1942 and again for part of 1944. He evidently enjoyed his time of peace and tranquillity here and it was said that he often slipped out of the gate of his 10-acre garden to enjoy a few holes of golf on Coombe Hill Golf Course situated behind the house.

General Dwight D Eisenhower, Commander-in-Chief of the Allied Forces during the Second World War and later President of the USA 1953-1961.

He lived for some months during the War at Telegraph Cottage (See also Page 51).

Many years later, when he was President of the United States, he came back to Coombe. This was undoubtedly a visit full of memories.

Map of 1940/1941 bombing in Coombe and parts of New Malden. Many people were killed and injured during these devastating raids which started on 16th August 1940.

The area around the railway junction was particularly hard-hit, as can be seen from this Map.

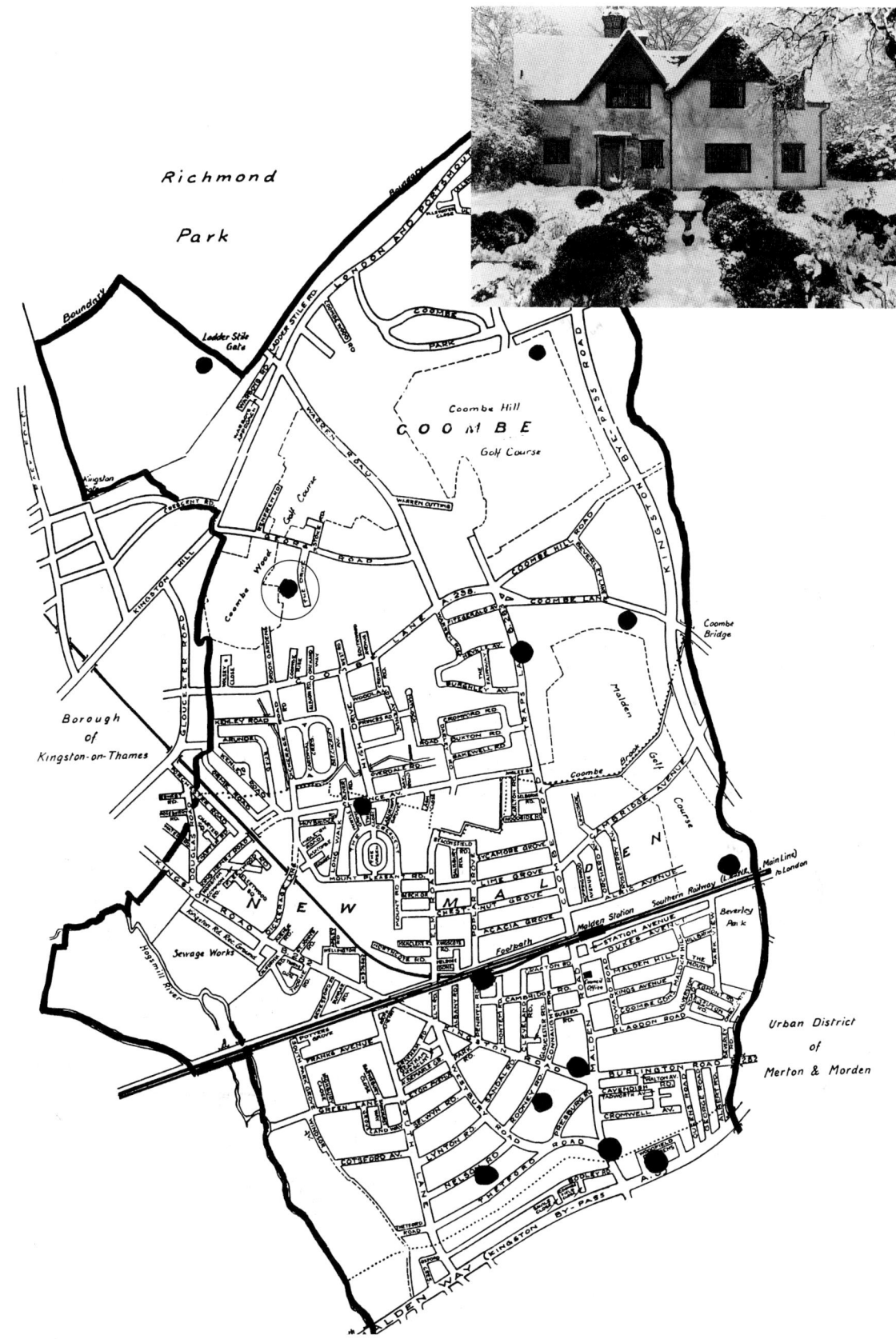

Telegraph Cottage, (inset photograph) was the sometime home of General Eisenhower during the War. This original house has now gone and a new development stands on the site.

The map shows the 1944 V1 bombing in Coombe and parts of New Malden.

Note that one of the bombs fell on the grounds of Coombe Ridge House.

ir Frederick died in 1949 and Coombe Ridge House was inherited by his sons. His beloved collection of artefacts, which had filled the house, were sold and by 1950 the house lay empty and neglected. The once beautiful gardens were left to become overgrown and wild.

Despite the fact that Sir Frederick had lavished money and attention on the house in earlier years, the ravages of time and war-damage (albeit comparitively minimal) meant that maintenance and repair work would need to be done to make it habitable.

Evidently the house was not easy to market as it remained unoccupied for nearly three years and by this time very few people were either willing, or able, to take on such a large property.

Some attempts were made to market the house during this period and Coombe Ridge House was advertised as 'An imposing Residence' in a 1951 'Country Life Magazine' Auction Advertisement. Apparently the house did not sell at this time and it was not until August of the following year that it was to finally change hands.

Front and rear photographs of the house in the early 1950's. It is interesting to compare these with those from the 1919 Auction Brochure on page 45 as they show how the house looked after the 1920's alterations.

The gardens, which had been so beautiful in the pre-War years, were a wilderness by the time this photograph was taken.

The new owners of Coombe Ridge House were the Roman Catholic Sisters of the Holy Family of Villefranche de Rouergue.

The Congregation originated in France in the 19th Century and was founded Emilie de Rodat, the daughter of a wealthy Catholic family from Villefranche in South-Western France. She founded a religious school for poor children in 1815 and from modest beginnings her teaching Congregation became established in France, the UK and many other countries.

By the late 1940's the Holy Family Sisters had a fee-paying school and Novitiate House, in Tooting. When these premises were adapted into a Secondary Modern School the Congregation needed to find a new home for their Junior School and Novitiate House. (The latter being a training intake for girls who wished to become Sisters).

After the purchase of Coombe Ridge House, parts of the building were adapted: one wing and the bedrooms on the top floor were reserved for the Sisters and the stable block and cottage housed the novitiates and the convent laundry.

The former Billiards Room became a Chapel and a special doorway was constructed out onto the Driveway so that the visiting Priest could enter and leave the building without needing to come into the main house. (Later on, this Chapel proved to be too small for the Sisters' needs and so the old Coach House at the other end of the building was converted into a larger Chapel).

As the Holy Family Sisters were a semi-enclosed community, visitors were restricted from entering certain parts of the building and in order that the Sisters could communicate with callers a grille was installed in the main door.

The Convent Chapel, now a classroom for some of the older girls of the school.

The window at the far end - behind the Altar - was the same one from which Mabel Galsworthy looked out onto the Rose Garden below, whilst her brothers played Billiards.

W hilst some parts of the house were being converted into a convent, other rooms were made ready for the arrival of the first pupils. The school officially opened in October 1952 with just 11 children.

(Before the house was converted into a Convent, Novitiate and School, the Sisters had to obtain Planning Permission from the local council. At the time when permission was granted, one of the clauses forbade the 'tolling of bells' - presumably so as not to annoy the neighbours!)

Right is the nursery classroom in the days when the School belonged to the Holy Family Sisters.

This room was formerly the Drawing Room of the house and at one time the large window that can be seen led into the Conservatory, which was demolished in the 1920's.

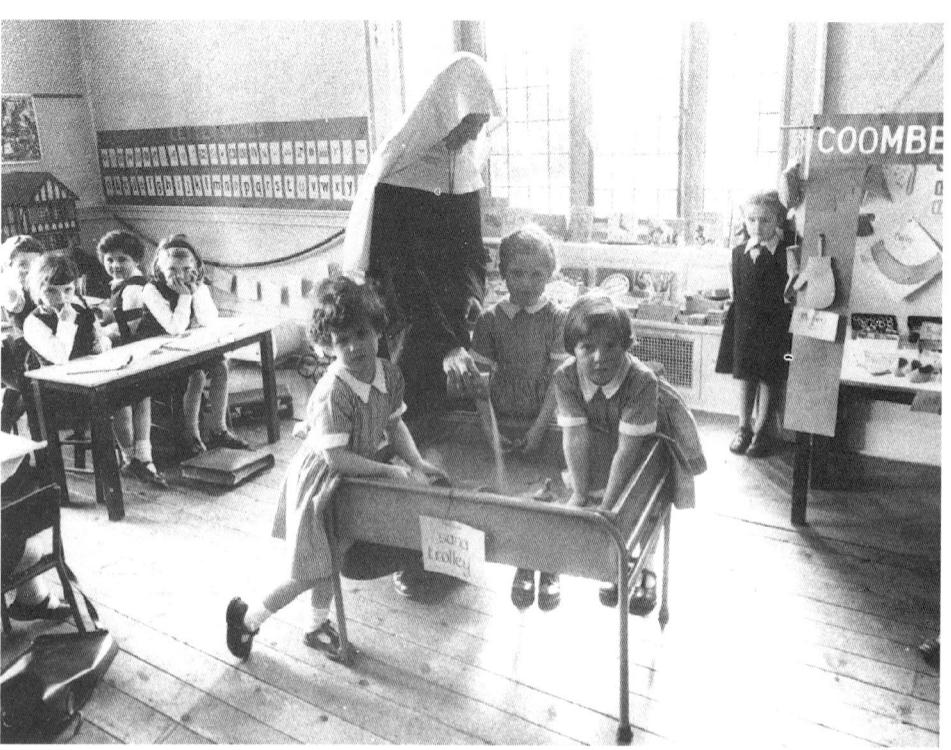

Right shows the Convent Kitchen which was situated in the original kitchen to the house. Here some of the Sisters are busy preparing a meal.

This room is also now a classroom situated opposite the Head Teacher's Office.

O ver the next 20 years the day-pupil numbers increased and for a short time there were also a few boarding girls.

More of the rooms were converted to classrooms and a new purpose-built hall was constructed on the lawns below the terrace. This necessitated the removal of the greenhouses which had stood against the garden walls since the house had first been built. Nevertheless, the Sisters still used some of the grounds for growing produce. The orchards yielded large amounts of fruit and there were chicken coops on the site of the old 'farm' for fresh eggs.

By the early 1970's, the Holy Family Sisters were needed elsewhere and it was decided that the Convent and Novitiate should move from Coombe. However the Sisters were anxious that the school should continue and were delighted when the nearby Community of Holy Cross Sisters decided to buy Coombe Ridge House.

At this time The Holy Cross Sisters already had a small preparatory

school in New Malden in a house called 'Keston', but were unable to expand this school further as a new convent had recently been built in the grounds.

Thus the two schools were amalgamated and Holy Cross Preparatory School opened on the 23rd September 1971.

Many of the Sisters and Novitiates who lived in Coombe recall how happy they were here, enjoying as they did the peace and tranquillity of the beautiful gardens.

These photos were taken before the new hall was built on the lawns. In the background of the lower picture are greenhouses, now demolished.

The stained glass window above the staircase was almost certainly installed some time after the house was altered in the 1920's, but we have never been able to identify who these men are.

In the hallway of Coombe Ridge House there is a beautiful stained glass window set high above the staircase, which contains the portraits of four rather serious looking gentlemen.

We believe that this window is not original to the house (the front wall of the hallway was moved back a few feet when the house was altered by Sir Frederick Pascoe Rutter in 1922) so we think that the window probably dates from around this time. However we have never been able to establish exactly who these men are.

It is possible that the two on the right are the Fitzgeorge Brothers, Augustus and Adolphus, who inherited the Coombe Estate from their father George, the second Duke of Cambridge.

Although the brothers inherited the Estate neither of them was able to succeed to the Royal title 'Duke of Cambridge'. Their father's marriage was considered invalid, under The Royal Marriages Act of 1772, by Queen Victoria who deemed his wife Louisa (an actress) to be an unsuitable consort for her cousin.

Consequently the Duke's children and descendants were unable to inherit the title and from then on the family were known as 'Fitzgeorge' (meaning 'son of...').

Although we do not know who they are, these gentlemen are lucky to have survived at all, as during the 1950's their portraits were covered over with black paint.

They were only revealed when the Holy Cross School had the window cleaned. Fortunately the paint that was used to obliterate them was of a washable variety and so today they stare down implacably at the children of the school as they skip up and down the staircase and corridors.......

The Holy Cross sisters are part of a world-wide order of Sisters founded in Switzerland in 1844 by Mother Bernarda Heimgartner and Father Theodosius.

The foundations for their order are firmly rooted in the teachings of St Francis of Assisi. Their apostolate encompasses working in the community and teaching.

The preparatory school at Coombe Ridge House is today one of three Holy Cross Schools in England; the others being an independent boarding school at Gerrards Cross and Holy Cross Secondary School in New Malden.

Coombe Ridge House was bought in the early 1970's by then Sister Provincial, Sister Bernarde (now Kathleen) Concagh and her abiding memory of the house at this time was that everywhere was painted brown! (Happily today the decor is somewhat less gloomy).

When the Holy Cross Preparatory School opened in 1971 the first Head Teacher was Sister Christina Crowe.

She was to remain as Head for the next 20 years.

Throughout this time Holy Cross Preparatory School has grown and flourished and there are now around 240 pupils, aged from 4 to 11 years, and more than 20 teachers.

The old house has been adapted and altered to accommodate the additional pupils. The servants' bedrooms on the second floor were converted to extra classrooms as were the stable block cottage, laundry and the Sisters' chapel (previously the old Coach House). The kitchen was converted into a classroom and what had once been the Butler's and Housekeeper's quarters now accommodate the Head Teacher and Bursar's Offices.

To comply with Fire Regulations an additional staircase up to the top floor had to be installed and the house rewired. Recently a new and expensive central heating replaced what was in parts a 70-year old system. In the 1970's a new Dining Hall was built and the Hall enlarged, connecting them both with the main house.

Since it opened in 1971 Holy Cross Preparatory School has grown and flourished.

This wonderful old house now echoes once again to the sound of children's voices.

57

Al Frescos and Frescoes...

Right : playtime in the gardens of Coombe Ridge House today as the children of Holy Cross Preparatory School take advantage of the wonderful open spaces.

Below: part of the Dining Room Mural that the Year 6 girls of 1994 painted - this part includes Mother Bernarda, founder of the Holy Cross Sisters.

The gardens too have been changed by necessity. In the lower grounds the apple and pear orchard was cleared to make way for the new Sports Field and running track.

On the second terrace, near to the Ivy Conduit House, there are netball and tennis courts and further up the garden there is new recreational equipment.

The former rose garden at the side of the house, which Blanche Galsworthy adored so much has also disappeared to make way for the Staff Car Park.

Yet despite all these 'changes' the gardens are today beautifully and lovingly maintained. The ornamental trees, which were planted so long ago, are flourishing and the flower beds are again filled with colour.

The view from Coombe Hill may have altered in the last few years, but the blue-grey ridge of the distant Surrey Downs can still be seen today.

The area around the house has seen many changes in the last few years. Local Government reorganisation in 1965 meant that the Borough of Malden and Coombe was amalgamated with Kingston and Surbiton to become part of the new enlarged Royal Borough of Kingston Upon Thames.

In the post-War years, many more houses have been built in Coombe and the surrounding area, providing some of the most exclusive and expensive housing estates and enclaves in the country.

Yet despite all this redevelopment the tree-lined roads, large gardens and the wide expanses of the golf courses still enable Coombe to retain an air of rural tranquillity and the views from the ridge of the hill remain as calming and inspirational as ever.

In the fading light of the evening, when the school has closed, a lull descends over the garden on the ridge of the hill.

The sound of the rustling trees echoes the whispers of the past.

Out of the shadows a cautious young vixen comes foraging for food.

She pauses, transfixed.....

The shrill cry of a night bird breaks her reverie.

The vixen turns.

Then like time itself she silently moves on into the gathering darkness....

60

Front Cover:
Original drawing of Coombe Ridge House c1875 by Ian Dunn.

Page 3 - Photo of Coombe Lane c1900 reproduced by courtesy of Kingston Museum and Heritage Service*.

Page 4 - Map of Coombe Estate c1837 reproduced by kind permission of KUTAS. Taken from Occasional Papers Number 3 by L Gent*.

Page 6 - Drawing of Ivy Conduit House today by Ian Dunn.

Page 9 -'Forsyte Saga' photograph by courtesy of the BBC Picture Archives. Reproduced with permission from the artistes.

Page 11 - Drawing of Bronze Age Village by Ian Dunn.

Page 13- Map of Conduit SystemWorks 34/103. Reproduced with permission from the Public Record Office.

Page 14 - Photographs of the interior of Coombe Conduit and Gallows Tamkin reproduced by permission of Surrey County Council Planning Department. Photograph of exterior of Coombe Conduit by permission of Kingston Museum and Heritage Service*.

Page 15 - External and internal photographs of Ivy Conduit House reproduced by kind permission of Surrey County Council Planning Office. Map of Bush Conduit Works 34/103 reproduced with permission from the Public Record Office.

Page 16 - Portrait of Earl Liverpool reproduced by courtesy of Kingston Museum and Heritage Service*.

Page 17 - Photograph of Coombe House reproduced by courtesy of Kingston Museum and Heritage Service*. Drawing of Coombe (Wood) House reproduced by courtesy of the Trustees of Sir John Soane's Museum, London.

Page 18 - Photograph of Coombe & Malden Flower Show 1909 reproduced by kind permission of Stephen Day, with thanks to Mrs Hurley.

Page 19 - Interior photographs of Coombe House reproduced by kind permission of RCHME (c) Crown Copyright.

Page 20 - Photo of The Fox and Coney reproduced by courtesy of Kingston Museum and Heritage Service*.

Page 22 - Drawing of the Coombe Wood Highwayman by Ian Dunn. Photograph of the Scarce Dagger Moth reproduced from 'The Moths and Butterflies of Great Britain and Ireland', Volume 10 with the kind permission of the publishers, Harley Books.

Page 23 - Illustration of the Duke of Cambridge by courtesy of Kingston Museum and Heritage Service*.

Page 24 - Photograph of Coombe Hill Farm House reproduced by permission of Surrey County Council Planning Department.

Page 25 - Map of Coombe Conduit System Works 34/104 reproduced with permission from the PRO. Photograph of Coombe Farm workers c1920 reproduced by permission of Kingston Museum and Heritage Service*.

Page 26 - Photograph of Coombe and Malden Station c1908 reproduced by permission of Kingston Museum and Heritage Service*.

Page 27 - Drawing of 'Robin Hill' by Ian Dunn.

Page 29 - Photograph of Coombe Warren reproduced with kind permission. Property of a private collection, New York.

Page 31- Coombe Road c1900 reproduced by permission of Kingston Museum and Heritage Service*. 'Forsyte Saga' reproduced by permission of the BBC Picture Library. We were unable to trace the artistes to ask their permission.

Index to Illustrations

J Allibone, 'George Devey Architect'.

William Bailey, 'The Surrey Highwaymen', The Surrey Magazine.

H C Butcher, 'Three Years With Eisenhower'.

Shaan Butters, 'The Book of Kingston'.

Father Michael Clifton, 'The Southwark Martyrs'.

Convent of the Holy Family, 'Saint Emilie de Rodat'.

Stephen H Day, 'Malden Old and New'.

Catherine Dupre ' John Galsworthy'.

Tim Everson, 'Kingston, Surbiton and Malden in Old Photographs'.

John Galsworthy: 'The Forsyte Saga', 'Glimpses and Reflections', 'A Motley'.

Norman Gash, 'The Life and Political Career of Robert Banks Jenkinson, 2nd Earl Liverpool 1770-1828'.

L Gent/Kingston upon Thames Archaeological Society: 'Occasional Papers Number III' entitled "The Manor of Coombe".

T W Holmes, 'The Semaphore'.

JW Lindus Forge, 'Hampton Court Water Supply', Surrey Arch.Society Vol LV1.

F Merryweather, 'Half a Century of Kingston History'.

RH Mottram, 'For Some We Loved'.

Peter Pugh, 'Absolute Integrity, the Story of Royal Insurance'.

Stuart Johnson Reid, 'Sir Richard Tangye'.

Mabel Reynolds, 'Memories of John Galsworthy'.

Sir Frederick Pascoe Rutter, 'The Twinkle'.

June Sampson, 'All Change, Kingston and Surbiton Old and New', plus articles in the 'Surrey Comet'.

Rudolf Sauter, 'Galsworthy the Man'.

John and Beryl Skelly, 'The Story of Chatley Heath Tower'.

Kay Sommersby Morgan, 'Past Forgetting'.

Richard South, 'The Moths of the British Isles'.

Sue Swales, Ian Yarham and Bob Britton, 'Nature Conservation in Kingston Upon Thames, London Ecology Unit'.

Joan Wakeford, 'Kingston's Past Rediscovered'.

I J West, 'Coombe Hill Farmhouse', Surrey Archaeological Collections, Vol LXIX.

John Weston, 'A History of Coombe Wood Golf Course'.

Mrs F Hwfa Williams, 'It Was Such Fun'.

B G Wilson, 'Conduit Houses at Coombe', Surrey County Journal.

Authorisations:

Quotations from the works of John Galsworthy were obtained by permission of the Society of Authors.

Quotations from the Surrey Comet were obtained by kind permission of the Editor.